B E T W E E N   T H E   G A T E S

Smyth & Helwys Publishing, Inc.
6316 Peake Road
Macon, Georgia 31210-3960
1-800-747-3016
©2006 by Smyth & Helwys Publishing
All rights reserved.
Printed in the United States of America.

The paper used in this publication meets the minimum requirements of
American National Standard for Information Sciences—
Permanence of Paper for Printed Library Materials.
ANSI Z39.48–1984. (alk. paper)

Library of Congress Cataloging-in-Publication Data

Poole, Charles E.
Between the gates / Charles E. Poole.
p. cm.
ISBN 1-57312-465-6 (pbk. : alk. paper)
1. Bible—Sermons.
2. Baptists—Sermons.
3. Sermons, American.
I. Title.
BS491.5.P66 2006
252'.061—dc22

2005037668

Between the Gates

HELPFUL WORDS FROM WHERE SCRIPTURE MEETS LIFE

BY CHARLES E. POOLE

Dedication

To
Marcia
Maria
Joshua and Anna

CONTENTS

PREFACE

Several years ago, in a televised interview, presidential biographer Edmund Morris was asked, "Why do you write?" Morris replied, "Because I can't *not* write."

I imagine that anyone who feels "called to write" would understand and even echo that answer. If you were born to write, you can't *not* write, which might be a bit of the truth traveling in that wonderful image Emily Dickinson gave us when she said, "I found a bird, this morning, down—down—on a little bush at the foot of the garden, and wherefore sing, I said, since nobody hears?" To which the bird replied, "My business is to sing." So it is with those who write. It is their business to write. They can't not write, even if no one ever hears or sees the words they have written.

But on those occasions when a writer's words are seen and heard, there are always others to be thanked and acknowledged because, while the necessity to write may have risen from deep within the writer, the words themselves are always shaped and formed by people and influences that are beyond and around the writer. Keenly aware of those influences and people who have formed my life, I now acknowledge debts too large to pay and too great to ignore.

I am grateful to editor Keith Gammons and his colleagues at Smyth & Helwys Publishing. Whenever my words have found their way into the light of day, it has been because of their interest, which now spans fifteen years. I am also grateful to Heather Gibson, who, with unfailing good cheer and patience, has typed my many pages of notebook paper onto a screen and out to a disk, overcoming my technological ineptness with her exceptional skills.

I am indebted to the LifeShare Foundation, a powerful witness to the love of God for those who struggle. Founded and sustained by the vision and generosity of Wayne and Zeita Parker, the LifeShare Foundation brings help and hope to people in need. I am privileged to serve as the foundation's community minister, a blessing for which I give thanks to God.

As a child, I was surrounded by adults who formed my life in wonderful ways at Log Cabin Baptist Church on Napier Avenue in Macon, Georgia. I will forever be in their debt. Later, in the decade of my twenties, "giants in the land" like Howard P. Giddens, W. Ches Smith III, and the late John W. Carlton became my mentors and guides. In my thirties, people such as Walter Shurden, Kirby Godsey, and Jim Bruner showed me the shape of theological and pastoral integrity, and First Church Macon folks like James and Miriam Trammell showed me the shape of authentic discipleship. In my forties, it was the people of First Baptist Church in Washington, D.C., and Northminster Baptist in Jackson, Mississippi, who continued to stretch and form me and mine. At every step along the way, our lives have been shaped by the church. Thanks be to God for the church.

And thanks be to God for family. No soul has ever owed more to family than I. My grandfathers, the late Charlie Cammack and Eugene Poole, whose total school years combined would not equal one elementary school education, filled my head with laughter that yet lives at the center of my soul. The Poole family into which I was born—my mother, father, and sister—loved me through everything I ever faced. The Smith family into which I married received me with unconditional grace, and the life Marcia and I share has sustained us both for now nearly thirty years. It is to Marcia, our daughter Maria, our son Joshua, and our daughter-in-law Anna that I dedicate this book, a small gesture of deep gratitude for so much love, laughter, strength, and joy.

I suffer from no illusion that anyone is interested in knowing who formed my life, but not to offer these words of gratitude would be to fail to acknowledge those who have shown me the way. The longer I live, the less enthusiasm I have for individualism. Nobody does anything, or even believes anything, all alone. Rather, we are formed, shaped, and sustained by the congregations that nurture us, the teachers who guide us, the friends who accept us, and the family that loves us. We all are deeply in debt to a long list of others. I am grateful for the privilege of a place on a page to acknowledge my many debts to those who have kindly shown me the way.

Charles E. Poole
Jackson, Mississippi

INTRODUCTION

Between the Gates

Almost everything that happens in the Bible happens somewhere between the gates. At one end of the Bible, a gate swings shut, never to be opened. At the other end of the Bible, a gate stands open, never to be closed. Almost everything else happens somewhere between the gates.

The closed gate gets shut early on, way back in Genesis. Adam and Eve have chosen to eat from the off-limits tree, despite God's warning that on the day they eat they will die. But, ominous warnings notwithstanding, they don't die. They don't lose their lives, but they do lose their place. Eden is over, never to be reclaimed. In Genesis 3:24, the gate to the garden closes behind Adam and Eve. God even puts a guard on the gate, a sure sign that there is no way back. Eden is closed. The garden is gone. The gate is shut. Forever.

But in the world of the Bible, when one gate closes, another one opens. Actually, another twelve: "The city has a great, high wall with twelve gates . . . on the east three gates, on the north three gates, on the south three gates and on the west three gates . . . . And the twelve gates are twelve pearls, each of the gates are a single pearl . . . and the gates will never be shut by day, and there will be no night there" (Rev

21:12-25). That's interesting: The gates are never closed in the day-time, and there is no night. Well, if they stay open all day, and night does not come, that must mean the gates never close. Ever. God's got a dozen gates, and none of them work! They are all stuck open, never to be closed.

I can't say for sure, but it might be worth noting that the open gates outnumber the closed gates twelve to one. One gate closed behind us but a dozen open before us might be a small sign of the great hope that there is much more joy ahead of us than there is pain behind us. One gate closed behind us and a dozen open in front of us might be a small sign of the great truth Jesus told his friends in John 16: "You have pain now, but I will see you again, and your hearts will rejoice, and no one will take your joy from you."

Like Adam and Eve before us, we all have a gate that is closed behind us, never to be opened. We have made choices we'd like to have back, and we have said words we'd like to take back. Life has turned out in ways we never would have planned. There's some of life we'd like to do over. But life doesn't come with a rewind button. Nobody gets to start over from the beginning. The gate to Eden is closed, never to be opened. Too much is too over. There is no pain in all the world like the pain of too late, the all-over pain of Eden's closed gate.

But because grace and hope are bigger and deeper than failure and disappointment, for every one gate that is closed behind us, never to be opened, there are a dozen open before us, never to be closed. There is more joy in front of us than there is pain behind us. God's welcome is never exhausted. God's grace never runs out. God's got gates, a dozen of them, and not a one of them will ever be closed.

We all live somewhere between the gates—between the pain of all that's over and the joy of all that's coming. One of the central tasks of pastoral preaching is to help people live truthful lives between the gates. A truthful life doesn't doll up the pain of all that's over and pretend there's nothing wrong, but neither does a truthful life lose sight of the hope and joy of the gospel of God. One of the great tasks of pastoral preaching is to help people honestly face the pain of all that's over and gladly embrace the joy of all that's coming.

That is some of what I seek to do in this book. I try to help people face the hard truth and embrace the glad truth. I also yearn to help people live with clarity, integrity, resolve, and hope. I seek to say a helpful word about the significance of family, the mystery of suffering, and the blessings to be found in a community of faith, and I hope to help people with the hard but necessary work of interpreting Scripture in conversation with, not in isolation from, the Bible's varied voices and persistent patterns.

Needless to say, these words come, as the words of preachers often do, from one struggling seeker to other struggling seekers, mindful that we're all stumbling away from a gate that is closed, never to be opened, on our way to a dozen standing open, never to be closed.

> There shall always be the Church and the World
> And the heart of Man
> Shivering and fluttering between them,
> choosing and chosen.
> Valiant, ignoble, dark and full of light
> Swinging between Hell Gate and Heaven Gate
> And the Gates of Hell shall not prevail.
> Darkness now, then light.
> —T. S. Eliot

CHAPTER 1

Adjusting

³⁶Then Jesus went with them to a place called Gethsemane; and he said to his disciples, "Sit here while I go over there and pray." ³⁷He took with him Peter and the two sons of Zebedee, and began to be grieved and agitated. ³⁸Then he said to them, "I am deeply grieved, even to death; remain here, and stay awake with me." ³⁹And going a little farther, he threw himself on the ground and prayed, "My Father, if it is possible, let this cup pass from me; yet not what I want but what you want." ⁴⁰Then he came to the disciples and found them sleeping; and he said to Peter, "So, could you not stay awake with me one hour? ⁴¹Stay awake and pray that you may not come into the time of trial; the spirit indeed is willing, but the flesh is weak." ⁴²Again he went away for the second time and prayed, "My Father, if this cannot pass unless I drink it, your will be done." (Matthew 26:36-42)

I couldn't believe my eyes. There it was, staring back at me from the twelve-items-or-less-lane. Perched in its usual spot, between the *T.V. Guide* and the *National Enquirer,* two racks above the Raisinets and Rolaids, was this week's edition of the *Weekly World News* (official motto: "The World's Only Reliable Newspaper"). The amazing thing about this particular edition was the headline. There it was in huge, urgent, earnest-looking letters: "GARDEN OF EDEN FOUND."

Needless to say, I did what any serious theologian would do; I moved into the express lane and purchased a copy of this stunning report. According to the article, soldiers on patrol in Iraq had stumbled across an ancient tree near Baghdad. Upon careful inspection they found, and I quote, "the skeletal remains of a large snake" and "a petrified apple . . . [that] looked as though two bites had been taken from it."[1] But wait. There's more. While retrieving the apple, the soldiers glimpsed the ghostly form of a woman whom they tentatively identified as Eve! The report concluded with the promise that the *Weekly World News* would keep us informed of any further developments.

But, alas, no further developments have been forthcoming. Indeed, *Weekly World News* headlines notwithstanding, there haven't been any further developments coming out of Eden for a long, long time. Ever since the gate closed behind Adam and Eve, Eden has been over. The gate is closed for good, and Eden is over forever. There is no going back to the perfect peace, security, joy, and innocence of Eden. Life has unfolded; time has moved on. Like Adam and Eve before us, we have all made choices and decisions that have left life less than perfect. Add to that life's natural losses and inevitable disappointments, and what you have is something other than Eden. Eden's gate is closed, and Eden's garden is gone. Too much is too over. We can't undo or take back or have back anything. We can only adjust to life as it is and seek, with the help of God, to live life after Eden as fully and faithfully as we can, because Eden will always be closed.

Which is why Gethsemane will always be open. If we can't find our way back to the garden of Eden, the only other garden to go to is Gethsemane. If we can't have the perfect peace and security of Eden, then we'll have to adjust to life as it is, come to terms with life outside of Eden, and trust God to help us live life fully and faithfully no matter what we have to face or bear. And that, of course, is where the other garden, Gethsemane, comes in.

Matthew, Mark, and Luke all record Jesus' visit to the garden of Gethsemane on the night before he died. Once he arrived in

Gethsemane, Jesus began praying for things to change: "And going a little farther, he threw himself on the ground and prayed, 'My Father, if it is possible, let this cup pass from me; yet not what I want but what you want'" (Matt 26:39). Jesus started out in Gethsemane praying for things to change, praying to be spared from the dreadful thing he was facing. Matthew 26:38-39 describes the depth of Jesus' sorrow: "Then he said to them, 'I am deeply grieved, even to death.' . . . And going a little farther he threw himself on the ground and prayed." Luke's Gospel reports that Jesus' anguish in Gethsemane was so intense that "His sweat became like great drops of blood" (Luke 22:44). Mark's record of that same night says Jesus was "distressed and agitated" (Mark 14:33). It is obvious that Jesus went to Gethsemane to pray as hard as a person can pray to be spared, to be delivered. Grieved to death, distressed, throwing himself to the ground, Jesus prayed with all his heart for God to remove the bitter cup he was about to drink.

But at some point during his visit to Gethsemane, Jesus adjusted his praying. His prayers moved from asking for things to change to accepting what he had to face. You can see it best in Matthew's account. In Matthew 26:39, Jesus prays, "My Father, if it is possible, let this cup pass from me; yet not what I want but what you want." Then, a little later, in Matthew 26:42, Jesus' prayer has moved from asking for things to change to accepting what cannot be changed: "My Father, if this cannot pass unless I drink it, your will be done." Jesus knows that the only way out is through the pain. He came to Gethsemane praying for God to get him around the awful pain, but he leaves Gethsemane trusting God to get him *through* the awful pain. In Gethsemane, Jesus' prayer moved from asking for things to change—"Take this cup from me"—to accepting what could not be changed—"If this cup cannot pass unless I drink it, your will be done."

Sooner or later, we all end up with Jesus, on our knees in Gethsemane, praying for God to get us around something we must go through. Like Jesus in Gethsemane, we pray that something will happen to spare us from the worst possible outcome and deliver us from the most awful darkness, sorrow, loss, and pain. If things always worked out that way, if we were given absolute immunity from heart-break and protection from sorrow, I guess we'd be back in Eden. But Eden is over. That garden is gone. All that's left is Gethsemane, the garden where we go to adjust, to accept the realities we face, to come to terms with what we must go through because we can't get around it. In November 1993, we learned that my father had a "spot on his liver." We all prayed as hard as we could that the spot would be benign. Then the biopsy results came back, and we had to adjust, praying instead that the cancer would be removable. When the surgery didn't work, we adjusted again and prayed that chemotherapy would help. When the chemotherapy failed, we adjusted our prayers to ask for Daddy to be comfortable. And at the end, we adjusted our prayers once more to pray that he would die peacefully. Sometimes, that's the way prayer moves. Sometimes prayer changes our lives, and sometimes life changes our prayers. Sometimes prayer changes the direction in which life is going, but sometimes prayer can only keep moving in an effort to catch up to life. Sooner or later we all find ourselves in Gethsemane. We start out praying for everything to be fine, and we end up coming to terms with what we must face, accepting realities we cannot change; adjusting, adjusting, adjusting.

Life is what it is, and it isn't Eden. That garden is gone. Life is frequently wonderful, often joyful, and usually good, but life is also sometimes painful, occasionally difficult, and at times heartbreaking. And all the praying in the world sometimes doesn't spare us from having to go through struggles we never imagined we would have to face. The poet Wendell Berry once wisely wrote, "We live the given life, not the planned." It's true. We can plan life as carefully as we please, but ultimately we live life in the shade of an if-shaped shadow. "If all goes well, we plan to do this. If we stay healthy, we hope to go there. If everything goes according to plan, we hope to do that." We live our lives in the hope-colored shade of an if-shaped shadow. The life we actually live is whatever life is given to us, which may or may not be the life we had planned. There will always be unwanted cups to drink and unplanned adjustments to make.

All of that is clear-eyed realism, and it is all true. But there is more to life than clear-eyed realism; there is also wide-eyed hope. After all, remember what happened to Jesus after he left Gethsemane. The bitter cup he dreaded turned out to be every bit as bad as he feared. His pain was awful. His suffering was terrible. And he died. But tragedy and death did not have the last word. The last word belonged to God. When God raised Jesus from the grave, God brought unimaginable joy, goodness, and triumph from unspeakable pain, sorrow, and loss.

And ever since, whenever anything has looked like a total loss and a terrible end, people have had to adjust their thinking to make room for hope.

Amen.

NOTE

[1] *Weekly World News* 26/49 (Boca Raton: American Media, Inc., 2001), 24.

CHAPTER 2

On Praying Through

²²*The same night he got up and took his two wives, his two maids, and his eleven children, and crossed the ford of the Jabbok.* ²³*He took them and sent them across the stream, and likewise everything that he had.* ²⁴*Jacob was left alone; and a man wrestled with him until daybreak.* ²⁵*When the man saw that he did not prevail against Jacob, he struck him on the hip socket; and Jacob's hip was put out of joint as he wrestled with him.* ²⁶*Then he said, "Let me go, for the day is breaking." But Jacob said, "I will not let you go, unless you bless me."* ²⁷*So he said to him, "What is your name?" And he said, "Jacob."* ²⁸*Then the man said, "You shall no longer be called Jacob, but Israel, for you have striven with God and with humans, and have prevailed."* ²⁹*Then Jacob asked him, "Please tell me your name." But he said, "Why is it that you ask my name?" And there he blessed him.* ³⁰*So Jacob called the place Peniel, saying, "For I have seen God face to face, and yet my life is preserved."* ³¹*The sun rose upon him as he passed Penuel,* limping because of his hip. *(Genesis 32:22-31, my emphasis)*

When I was a college student I was, for a brief period of time, the baritone singer in a gospel quartet. We traveled around rural Georgia, singing in small churches and school auditoriums. While we never became sufficiently successful to acquire one of those buses with our name painted on the fenders, we did manage to obtain some look-alike outfits—dark brown double-knit leisure suits with wide-collar, floral-print, tropical-looking shirts (sort of UPS meets Hawaii Five-O).

My travels as a gospel singer took me outside my closely guarded Baptist world into the foreign orbit of Pentecostal, Nazarene, and Assembly of God churches where I sometimes heard a phrase with which I had been previously unfamiliar. The phrase was "praying through." The people in those churches were fond of saying they had "prayed through," and they were quick to urge others to "pray through," a simple way of encouraging someone to hold on, not to give up, to keep on praying until peace or resolution or relief came.

If anyone ever embodied the truth that travels in those two words, "praying through," it was Jacob by the Jabbok, wrestling for a blessing all night long. Whatever else this story is about, it is at least a story about holding on and praying through. "I have to go now," says the stranger. "Not so fast," says Jacob. "You aren't going anywhere until you bless me. I'm holding on and I am not about to let go." In the words of those old Pentecostal saints, Jacob was determined to "pray through." He would not let go and he did not let go until he received a blessing from the one with whom he was wrestling.

Of course, careful speech requires us to say that we don't know exactly with whom Jacob was wrestling. The story doesn't come right out and identify the one with whom Jacob struggles on the creek bank. Genesis 32:34 says, "A man wrestled with Jacob until daybreak." But as the sun rose, Jacob said, "I have seen God face to face." So with whom was Jacob wrestling? A man? An angel? Himself? God? The story leaves us in the dark as to the identity of the all-night stranger, but the weight of the evidence seems to suggest that Jacob was wrestling with God: "Then the man said, 'You shall no longer be called Jacob, but Israel, for you have wrestled with God and with humans and have prevailed.' And there he blessed him. So Jacob called the name of the place Peniel, saying, 'I have seen God face to face.'"

For those who have ever had to pray their way through a dark and desperate time, Jacob's wrestling sounds like our praying, the kind of holding-on-to-God praying my Pentecostal friends had in mind when they talked about "praying through." Jacob's all-night, life-or-death, holding-on-for-a-blessing wrestling with God is a rough-and-tumble picture of the principle Jesus gave us when he said, "Ask and it shall be given to you, seek and you will find, knock and the door will be opened to you." There is a persistent kind of praying that asks, seeks, knocks; asks, seeks, knocks; asks, seeks, knocks day after day after night after night. We pray and we pray and we pray, holding on for the guidance or relief or help or courage we seek, praying, praying, praying for the son or daughter or husband or wife or friend or brother or sister to be healed or changed or helped or stopped or spared. We are Jacob, wrestling for the blessing. We will not let go, because we cannot let go. There is nothing else to do but pray, because there is nowhere else to go but God.

Such talk raises the inevitable pragmatic question, "Does our persistent praying and relentless wrestling actually change outcomes?" We have to be careful how we approach that most practical of all questions about prayer, the "Does it work?" question. On the one hand, there is the popular, easy answer that "prayer changes things," which finds an apparent biblical guarantee in verses such as "If you ask anything of the Father in my name, you will receive it" (John 15:7, 16). That sounds so certain, so final, so sure. But then comes the day when we bury the young person we prayed for in Jesus' name. Then what? Then some would say we didn't pray with enough faith or hard enough or long enough. That idea doesn't ring true, because it seems to suggest that God has established a minimum required amount of time and intensity for answerable prayer, without revealing to us the rules, and that doesn't sound like God. Or, another popular answer is to say that God sometimes says "No," sometimes says "Yes," sometimes says "Wait," which sounds reasonable enough, but that is not what the Gospel of John suggests when it says, "If you ask anything of the Father in my name, you will receive it."

There is mystery here, much mystery. The mystery keeps us from saying too much about how prayer "works." But, on the other hand, we mustn't allow the mystery to cause us to believe too little about the difference prayer makes in the world. I don't go around saying "prayer changes things," but I do go around believing that prayer changes things. I have prayed for mountains to move that stayed put, but I have also seen hurting people and difficult circumstances prayed through to a good conclusion and a genuine transformation. The longer I live, the more I know that we must be as careful not to say too little about prayer as we are not to say too much about prayer. The fact is, "praying without ceasing," holding on and praying through, does make a real difference in tough situations and in the people for whom we pray. Of course, even that much must be said with care and restraint, lest we begin to see prayer as a way to manage God and other people. ("If I pray hard enough and long enough, I can get God to come around and do my will." "If I pray for her long enough, God will make her act the way I want her to." "If I pray for him hard enough, God will make him come around and agree with me.") This much mystery requires us to take great care, lest we say too much about the certainty of prayer. But, on the other hand, this much wonder requires us to take equal care lest we say too little about the power of prayer.

In the face of all that mystery and wonder, one thing we can say with absolute confidence is that persistent, constant, never-let-go praying changes the one who is doing the praying. Jacob's long night of prayer did not change what he had to face. When the sun came up, he still had to go meet Esau. But though his situation was not changed, Jacob was. As the sun rose on Jacob, he came limping over the hill. Everyone who knew him could see the difference in the way he was walking after all that wrestling. As the night of long struggle changed Jacob, the life of constant prayer changes us. Constant praying, praying through, can leave us with a good limp; not as quick, not so fast, less noisy, less angry, less arrogant, kinder, more quiet, more thoughtful. The life of constant prayer can color, shape, strengthen, and soften our lives in pure, good, and peaceful ways. In fact, it not only can; it will.

There is much mystery here, like the midnight mystery in which Jacob wrestled with himself, his fears, his longings, and God. At the heart of the mystery, though, is the blessing; sometimes the blessing of a changed situation, always the blessing of our own changed, deepened, softened, strengthened life. So hold on. Don't let go. Pray through.

Amen.

CHAPTER 3

Through the Valley

¹The LORD is my shepherd, I shall not want. ²He makes me lie down in green pastures; he leads me beside still waters; ³he restores my soul. He leads me in right paths for his name's sake. ⁴Even though I walk through the darkest valley, I fear no evil; for you are with me; your rod and your staff—they comfort me. ⁵You prepare a table before me in the presence of my enemies; you anoint my head with oil; my cup overflows. ⁶Surely goodness and mercy shall follow me all the days of my life, and I shall dwell in the house of the LORD my whole life long. (Psalm 23:1-6)

Sometimes when I hear the sentence at the center of Psalm 23, the one about going through the valley of the shadow of death, it takes me back to a sermon William Sloane Coffin preached after the tragic, sudden death of his son. In his sermon, Dr. Coffin said that what God had given the Coffin family, in this particular case, was "minimum protection and maximum support." They had not been protected from the worst grief they could imagine, but they had been sustained by more strength than they could explain, leading Dr. Coffin to the conclusion that, sometimes, what God gives people is "minimum protection and maximum support."[1]

If you've lived a life that has been troubled only by natural losses and normal struggles, that might not ring true to you. You might feel extremely "protected" by God. You may feel that what God gives is not only maximum support, but maximum protection also. If, on the other hand, your world has ever been shattered by a grief too great to bear, if you are living with a terrible struggle that never goes away, if you have borne one burden after another until your life has come to feel like one long, steep, dark valley of the shadow of death, then you might have just found the words you've always been aching for: "God gave us minimum protection and maximum support."

In the sentence at the center of the psalm, the psalmist does not suggest that having the Lord as our shepherd will somehow keep us from having to go through the darkest valley of them all. "Yea, though I walk through the valley of the shadow of death, I will fear no evil, for thou art with me. Thy rod and thy staff, they comfort me" (Ps 23:4, KJV). The sentence at the center of the psalm seems to say that, while God's presence does not protect us from every sad reality, God's presence will support us in every hard struggle. In the valley of the dark shadows, God is with us, enabling us to live through things that, if someone had told us ahead of time we were going to have to live through, we would have sworn we could never do it. But, somehow, we do. With the help of God and with the strength we draw from the people of God, we stay on our feet and keep moving. We are able to go through what could not be gotten around, because even when we don't get maximum protection, we do get maximum support.

I believe God sometimes spares us and protects us. (Of course, we usually don't know from what we have been protected, because the bad thing from which God protected us didn't happen to us because God protected us from it. Thus, we don't know what it was!) But I also know that God does not protect us from all tragedy, heartache, and sorrow. And it is then, when we are not protected, that we are supported.

Complete protection or sustaining support. Given the choice, we would always take the first. But when we don't get the first, we do receive the second. Even when we don't get enough protection to keep us out of the valley of the shadow of death, we do get enough support to get us through it.

Amen.

NOTE

[1] From "Alex's Death" in *A Chorus of Witnesses*, eds. Thomas G. Long and Cornelius Platinga, Jr. (Grand Rapids: Wm. B. Eerdmans, 1994), 265.

CHAPTER 4

From Suffering

¹Therefore, since we are justified by faith, we have peace with God through our Lord Jesus Christ, ²through whom we have obtained access to this grace in which we stand; and we boast in our hope of sharing the glory of God. ³And not only that, but we also boast in our sufferings, knowing that suffering produces endurance, ⁴and endurance produces character, and character produces hope, ⁵and hope does not disappoint us, because God's love has been poured into our hearts through the Holy Spirit that has been given to us. ⁶For while we were still weak, at the right time Christ died for the ungodly. ⁷Indeed, rarely will anyone die for a righteous person—though perhaps for a good person someone might actually dare to die. ⁸But God proves his love for us in that while we still were sinners Christ died for us. (Romans 5:1-8)

Suffering rarely receives such warm reviews as those Paul assigns it in Romans 5:3: "We rejoice in our sufferings, because suffering produces endurance, endurance produces strength, and strength produces hope." That's about as lofty an assessment of suffering as we are likely to find.

And it's true, of course. Suffering does transform our lives in ways that comfort rarely does. A few of us may have been changed by comfort and joy, but more of us have grown through suffering and pain. This is perhaps what the psalmist meant by these words in Psalm 119:71: "It is good for me that I have been afflicted." The suffering we endure does somehow open us up to God in ways beyond the reach of comfort and joy. For making us deeper, kinder, stronger, and softer, pain often carries more weight and usually does more good than joy. So, of course, when we read Paul's words in Romans 5, "We rejoice in suffering, because suffering produces endurance, endurance produces character, and character produces hope," we recognize them as true. From suffering, good does come.

But we have to be careful here, because if we aren't careful we will romanticize suffering by turning it into a nice gift that always leads to good things. We have to be careful not to doll up suffering and trouble and pain. When, for example, we read those words from Romans 5, "Suffering produces endurance, endurance produces character, and character produces hope," we must read them quietly and reverently, remembering all our sisters and brothers for whom the suffering became so deep and so dark that they lost all hope that life would ever be bearable or livable again and, in that depth of despair, chose to end their own lives. For some of our sisters and brothers, suffering did not produce endurance. For some, the darkness of suffering became unbearable, and in their agony they ended their lives. May they find, in God's unhindered presence, the peace and relief that was not theirs in this life. When we read Paul's optimistic words about how endurance, strength, and hope all come from suffering, we have to read them quietly, not gleefully; reverently, not glibly; knowing that the good outcome Paul assigns to suffering is not automatic. Pain hurts, and for some of our sisters and brothers, the pain of life is deeper than any of us will ever know.

It is only after we have acknowledged the shadows that gather around Romans 5:3 that we are ready to embrace the light that shines in Romans 5:3, the light of hope for those who suffer: "We rejoice in suffering, because suffering produces endurance, endurance produces character, and character produces hope." Those words tell us that the suffering we endure really can transform our lives. We can emerge from suffering stronger, kinder, and deeper. It isn't automatic, but it is possible.

Indeed, it is God's nature to bring from suffering some surprising goodness that no one ever could have imagined in the depth of the darkness and pain. That does not mean God sends us the suffering to make us better. The suffering comes because we live in a world where bad things happen. That's why the suffering comes. There is a long list of ways that things can go wrong in life. From some of them God spares us, thanks be to God. But most of us will suffer in some way, not because God sent the suffering, but because that is the nature of life. But when the suffering comes, it is God's nature to wring unimaginable good from unspeakable pain.

Our calling is not to get over our pain. Our calling is to get through our pain and be changed by it. The depth and strength we gain from our pain is not something we would want to get over. The depth and strength we gain from our pain are the leftovers that remain; the costly gifts that come only from suffering. Paul described those gifts that come from suffering as endurance, character, and hope. If suffering can produce such life-transforming gifts as those, we would not want to "get over it." Instead, we need only to get through it and then hold on to the sacred leftovers of our suffering. I have not had to bear much pain in my life, but the sorrows and struggles I have known have always left me kinder, quieter, more thoughtful, and more compassionate. So, while I know how important it is for us to get through our suffering, I know that it is equally important for us not to get over it.

After all, if Paul is right, if suffering produces so much that is so good, who would ever want to "get over it" and go back to being who they were before their life was deepened, softened, and strengthened by the pain and the struggle? In the face of our suffering, then, let us learn to pray, "O God, help me to live through this and move beyond this, but please don't ever let me get over whatever gifts I gain from this suffering."

Amen.

CHAPTER 5

From Agony to Memory to Story

¹*After these things God tested Abraham. He said to him, "Abraham!" And he said, "Here I am." ²He said, "Take your son, your only son Isaac, whom you love, and go to the land of Moriah, and offer him there as a burnt offering on one of the mountains that I shall show you." ³So Abraham rose early in the morning, saddled his donkey, and took two of his young men with him, and his son Isaac; he cut the wood for the burnt offering, and set out and went to the place in the distance that God had shown him. ⁴On the third day Abraham looked up and saw the place far away. ⁵Then Abraham said to his young men, "Stay here with the donkey; the boy and I will go over there; we will worship, and then we will come back to you." ⁶Abraham took the wood of the burnt offering and laid it on his son Isaac, and he himself carried the fire and the knife. So the two of them walked on together. ⁷Isaac said to his father Abraham, "Father!" And he said, "Here I am, my son." He said, "The fire and the wood are here, but where is the lamb for a burnt offering?" ⁸Abraham said, "God himself will provide the lamb for a burnt offering, my son." So the two of them walked on together. ⁹When they came to the place that God had shown him, Abraham built an altar there and laid the wood in order. He bound his son Isaac, and laid him on the altar, on top of the wood. ¹⁰Then Abraham*

reached out his hand and took the knife to kill his son. ¹¹*But the angel of the*
LORD called to him from heaven, and said, "Abraham, Abraham!" And he said,
"Here I am." ¹²*He said, "Do not lay your hand on the boy or do anything to*
him; for now I know that you fear God, since you have not withheld your son,
your only son, from me." ¹³*And Abraham looked up and saw a ram, caught in*
a thicket by its horns. Abraham went and took the ram and offered it up as a
burnt offering instead of his son. ¹⁴*So Abraham called that place "The LORD*
will provide"; as it is said to this day, "On the mount of the LORD it shall be
provided." (Genesis 22:1-14)

Rarely have so many questions traveled in such small space. There may
not be another page in the whole Bible that spawns as many questions
per square inch as the story of Abraham and Isaac on Mount Moriah.

For starters, there is verse 1, which says God decided to test
Abraham. Does that mean the afflictions that come to people in life
are "tests," sent to us from God to find out what we are made of?
Would that include spinal cord injuries that leave children paralyzed
and drive-by shootings that kill preschoolers? Are those tests? Which
tragedies are "tests from God," and which come only because we live
in a world of trouble? Or is it that we only come later to look upon
our past troubles as "tests," because when we look back on them we
know our faith and strength truly were tested? Those are a few questions Genesis 22 raises, and we're still in verse 1—"God tested
Abraham."

Then there is verse 12, in which God says, "Now I know that you
fear the Lord, since you have not withheld your only son from me."
Now God knows? That means prior to the moment Abraham raised
the knife, God did not know. But what about the idea that God
knows everything that's going to happen before it happens?

Those are just a couple of theological questions that travel around
in Genesis 22. There are also a few personal, pastoral, human questions. For example: Would the God who is revealed in Jesus tell a
parent to bring a child to the brink of death? And what about Isaac?
How did the sight of his own father raising a knife above him affect
Isaac? And what about Abraham? What sort of internal conflict must
have been raging inside Abraham? Did he question his own sanity?

Did he wonder if the voice that told him to sacrifice Isaac was really the voice of God? What was going on inside Abraham as he climbed Mt. Moriah with a knife in his hand, a child in his shadow, and a lump in his throat?

The text, of course, does not answer these questions, because it does not ask them. The text is not bothered by such questions as these. The text is about Abraham's obedient trust in God and God's unfailing provision in response to Abraham's unwavering trust. What was perhaps at the time a moment of unbearable agony for Abraham eventually became a story with a single, central message: "God can be trusted." Abraham's agony is no longer evident. All that's left is the story.

That is the basic movement of life for all of us. When we are facing a dreadful difficulty or enduring a hard struggle or bearing an unbearable sorrow, the agony can be paralyzing. While we are in it, we don't think we can live through it. But we do. We do live through it. Time passes. Life moves on. And eventually, the unbearable agony becomes a painful memory. And later, perhaps after we're gone, the painful memory becomes a sacred story, just as Abraham's unbearable agony eventually became Isaac's painful memory and finally became our sacred story. It may have been unbearable to be Abraham that day he climbed Mt. Moriah with a knife in one hand and a son in the other, but now it's just letters on a page, sounds in the air: "God told Abraham to sacrifice Isaac, and Abraham obeyed because he trusted God." All that agony, and now it's just a story.

That's the way life moves. Every unbearable agony eventually becomes a painful memory and finally a sacred story. Alfred Tennyson's world was torn asunder by the sudden death of his friend Arthur Hallam in 1833. For Tennyson, who had already endured much sorrow, Hallam's death was a terrible agony. Eventually he began to write about that agony, which had become by then a painful memory. Now, whenever high school kids study Tennyson's great poem "In Memoriam," all of that sorrow is just a story they learn so they'll know why Tennyson wrote, "Forgive my grief for one removed, Thy creature whom I found so fair."[1] All that agony, and now it isn't even anybody's memory; it's just everybody's story.

In the book *Lincoln's Melancholy,* Joshua Wolf Shenk quotes from a letter Abraham Lincoln wrote to a friend in 1841, in which Lincoln, paralyzed in the depths of long depression, wrote, "I am now the most miserable man living. If what I feel were equally distributed to the whole human family, there would not be one cheerful face on the earth. Whether I shall ever be better I cannot tell; I awfully forebode I shall not. To remain as I am is impossible; I must die or be better."[2] That was Lincoln's unbearable agony, episodes of depression from which he felt he would never emerge. All that agony, and now it isn't even anybody's memory; it's just everybody's story.

That's the way life moves, from agony to memory to story. The long struggles, the haunting depressions, the tragic losses, every crushing betrayal, every long separation, every bitter divorce, every paralyzing fear, every devastating death; they all start out as unbearable agony. With the passage of time, the unbearable agony becomes a painful memory. Years and years later, all that's left is the sacred story. The eventual echo is always softer than the original sound.

My mother had a twin brother who died as a baby. At the time, it was a terrible agony for her parents. By the time I came along, his death had faded from unbearable agony to painful memory for my grandparents. Now it's a story that comes up every few years at Christmas. How does that happen? How does something that is so unbearable eventually become a memory and, finally, a story? It has something to do, or everything to do, with time. At the time you are going through a terrible heartbreak, the days crawl. Years later, when you look back on it, those crawling days of your pain are just part of the flying years of your life. Present tense, the hard days crawl. Past tense, they flew. The unbearable agony becomes a painful memory. Then we die, and all that remains is the sacred story.

That is the way life moves: from agony to memory to story. We live through something so terrible that if someone had told us ahead of time we were going to have to face it, we would have sworn we could never live through it. But we do. We do live through the worst kinds of agony. And, eventually, the unbearable agony becomes a painful memory, and, finally, a sacred story.

For people of faith, the point of all those stories is always the same. For people of faith, the point of all the stories about all the agonies is always the same: The Lord will provide. If the Lord doesn't provide a way around the agony, the Lord does provide a way through. God does exactly what Abraham told Isaac God would do: "The Lord will provide." It is true. Otherwise we would not have lived through the agonies we could not go around. But we have lived through and come out, and what once was an unbearable agony is now a painful memory, and someday it will be a story our children will tell their children around the supper table. Our unbearable agony will just be sounds in the air, words in a room. The eventual echo will be much softer than the original sound, but that is all it can be, because that is the way life moves; from agony to memory to story. And the point of all the stories about all the agonies is always the same: God can be trusted. The Lord will provide. (We know that it is so. Otherwise, we would never have lived to tell the story.)

Amen.

NOTES

[1] Alfred Tennyson, *In Memoriam*, ed. Robert H. Ross (New York: W.W. Norton and Company, 1973), 4.

[2] Joshua Wolf Shenk, *Lincoln's Melancholy* (New York: Houghton Mifflin Company, 2005), 62.

CHAPTER 6

The Palm Sunday Principle

²⁸After he had said this, he went on ahead, going up to Jerusalem. ²⁹When he had come near Bethphage and Bethany, at the place called the Mount of Olives, he sent two of the disciples, ³⁰saying, "Go into the village ahead of you, and as you enter it you will find tied there a colt that has never been ridden. Untie it and bring it here. ³¹If anyone asks you, 'Why are you untying it?' just say this, 'The Lord needs it.'"³²So those who were sent departed and found it as he had told them. ³³As they were untying the colt, its owners asked them, "Why are you untying the colt?"³⁴They said, "The Lord needs it."³⁵Then they brought it to Jesus; and after throwing their cloaks on the colt, they set Jesus on it. ³⁶As he rode along, people kept spreading their cloaks on the road. ³⁷As he was now approaching the path down from the Mount of Olives, the whole multitude of the disciples began to praise God joyfully with a loud voice for all the deeds of power that they had seen, ³⁸saying, "Blessed is the king who comes in the name of the Lord! Peace in heaven, and glory in the highest heaven!"³⁹Some of the Pharisees in the crowd said to him, "Teacher, order your disciples to stop."⁴⁰He answered, "I tell you, if these were silent, the stones would shout out."⁴¹As he came near and saw the city, he wept over it, ⁴²saying, "If you, even you, had only recognized on this day the things that make for peace! But now they are hidden from your eyes. ⁴³Indeed, the days will come upon you, when your enemies will set up ramparts around you and surround you, and hem you in on

every side. ⁴⁴*They will crush you to the ground, you and your children within*
you, and they will not leave within you one stone upon another; because you
did not recognize the time of your visitation from God." (Luke 19:28-44)

Have you ever seen so much joy in such close proximity to so much
pain? You watch those palms waving and you see that crowd rejoicing
and you hear those voices singing, but you know what's just around
the bend. You know what's going to happen before the week is over,
and it makes you wonder if so much joy has ever landed so near to so
much pain. Indeed, the Palm Sunday singing was so joyful and the
Palm Sunday crowd so loud that the authorities told Jesus to make the
people calm down and be quiet. But Jesus told the authorities that
something so wonderful and joyful was happening here that if the
people didn't sing, the rocks would. It was a day of that much joy. And
yet, the deepest pain was just around the corner. The Palm Sunday
parade would soon fade, and what came next would be Judas' betrayal,
Peter's denial, Gethsemane's tears, Friday's cross, and Jesus' death.
Hard losses, dark shadows, deep struggles, and thick grief would fill
the last week of Jesus' life. But the first day of the last week was this
song-singing, high-stepping, palm-waving day of unrestrained and
unrestrainable gladness. Has so much joy ever been found in such
close proximity to so much pain?

The answer, of course, is "yes." It happens that way all the time.
Joy and pain have always lived in the same neighborhood, on the same
street, at the same address. Holy Week's compression of high joy and
deep pain into small space looks a lot like real life in the real world.
We live in a world where there is more pain than any meter can measure. If a broken heart could kill you, we'd all be dead.
Disappointment, depression, and anxiety haunt the rich and the poor.
Disease, malnutrition, and war fill hospitals and graveyards.
Manipulation and misunderstanding fracture families and scar relationships. Dreams have to be buried, plans have to be forsaken,
compromises have to be made, and hopes have to be trimmed because
life takes hard turns we didn't count on and couldn't control. There is
a long list of ways that things can go wrong in life. There is a lot of
pain. But if there is a lot of pain, there is also a lot of joy. The joy gets

lost more easily than the pain, though, because pain weighs more than joy. Pain has more gravity than joy has helium. That may be what Lewis Grizzard had in mind when he said, "Losing feels worse than winning feels good."[1] Perhaps that's what Lord Byron hinted at when he wrote, "Earth gives no joy like that it takes away." It's probably part of the truth behind Frederick Buechner's observation that "Parents are only as happy as their unhappiest child."[2] That's the gravity of pain. We are only as happy as the unhappiest person we love because pain weighs more than joy.

The temptation, of course, is to sacrifice joy on the altar of pain, to call off Palm Sunday's parade because you know it's only taking you that much nearer to Good Friday's cross. The temptation is to play down the joy because you know it isn't going to last. The temptation is to echo Burley in Wendell Berry's novel *A Place on Earth*, when Burley laments, "To celebrate things ain't hardly bearable, because they won't always stay celebratable."[3] But those are temptations to be resisted. We mustn't play down the joy, no matter how much pain is on the way. When the Pharisees said, "Turn down the music," Jesus said, "If the people don't sing the rocks will." That is the Palm Sunday principle: When it's time to be glad, it's time to be glad. Today's joy must not be sacrificed on the altar of tomorrow's pain. Joy is as real as pain, and as surely as pain must be endured, joy must be enjoyed.

A few years ago, at the age of forty-seven, I went to my first prom. If you've never been to one, I hope you get to someday. They had decorations and pretty lights and a real band, and the dads and daughters had the first dance. The band was playing arguably the greatest song in the history of Western civilization. ("I've got sunshine on a cloudy day, and when it's cold outside, I've got the month of May.") In the midst of it all, for one brief shimmering splinter of a moment, I looked around that room at all those happy families. Because families are what families are, I knew a lot of pain and worry and fear had been left at the door. And I knew when it came time for all those families to go home from the prom, many of them would be driving back into pain as surely as Jesus drove his donkey from the Palm Sunday parade toward the Good Friday cross. But for that one moment, it was time to be nothing but glad. To look around that room, you would've never guessed that there was an ounce of agony in Jackson or Baghdad or anywhere in between. The prom was, for a shiny moment, a tiny parable of the Palm Sunday principle that today's joy must not be sacrificed on the altar of tomorrow's pain.

There is plenty of pain around us and inside us. There is a lot about which to be sad and worried and afraid. But when it's time to be glad, it's time to be glad. As surely as pain, when it comes, must be endured, joy, when it is here, must be enjoyed. And anyway, the truth is that we were made, not for pain, but for joy. Ultimately, it will be joy, not pain, that has the last word. The ultimate sign that joy, not pain, will have the last word is something that is going to happen next week. Something stunning is going to happen, and the pain and death of Good Friday is going to give way to the joy of . . .

Well, I don't want to spoil the surprise, so I'm just going to stop with that. But, you come back next weekend and you'll see.

Amen.

NOTES

[1] From a Lewis Grizzard column in the *Atlanta Journal-Constitution*, n.d.

[2] Long ago I read this sentence in one of Frederick Buechner's books; I know not which one.

[3] Wendell Berry, *A Place on Earth* (Washington, D.C.: Centerpoint, 2001), 290.

CHAPTER 7

At the Annual Easter Dance

*¹After the sabbath, as the first day of the week was dawning, Mary Magdalene
and the other Mary went to see the tomb. ²And suddenly there was a great
earthquake; for an angel of the Lord, descending from heaven, came and rolled
back the stone and sat on it. ³His appearance was like lightning, and his clothing white as snow. ⁴For fear of him the guards shook and became like dead
men. ⁵But the angel said to the women, "Do not be afraid; I know that you are
looking for Jesus who was crucified. ⁶He is not here; for he has been raised, as
he said. Come, see the place where he lay. ⁷Then go quickly and tell his disciples, 'He has been raised from the dead, and indeed he is going ahead of you to
Galilee; there you will see him.' This is my message for you." ⁸So they left the
tomb quickly with fear and great joy, and ran to tell his disciples. ⁹Suddenly
Jesus met them and said, "Greetings!" And they came to him, took hold of his
feet, and worshiped him. ¹⁰Then Jesus said to them, "Do not be afraid; go and
tell my brothers to go to Galilee; there they will see me." (Matthew 28:1-10)*

It is reported that, on an Easter Sunday morning more than sixty years
ago, Harry Emerson Fosdick climbed into the pulpit of New York
City's Riverside Church, gazed out at the congregation, and said, "It's
a great year for Easter."¹ It was, in fact, a frightening year to be alive.
World War II was raging. Thousands were dying across the seas. Pearl

Harbor's shadow still lay large across a grieving nation. It was an ominous and uncertain time in every corner of the world. Which, of course, made Fosdick's words ring especially true. It was an unusually great year for Easter, because the darker the days and the more frightening the times, the more hungry we are to fall into Easter's arms.

The more difficult our lives become, the more we ache for the hope we find in Easter's arms. We fall into Easter's arms to be held up and held near by the comfort and hope of Easter's annual reminder that the future belongs to God. No matter how dark or painful or hopeless life seems, God always has something else, something good, something completely new yet to do. That is the truth we find in Easter's arms. When Jesus died on Friday, no one thought there was going to be a resurrection. Jesus' friends didn't go to the cemetery on Sunday morning to celebrate a resurrection; they went to embalm a body. But once they got there, they discovered that what looked like the end of everything good had become, instead, the beginning of something new,[2] something they never would have dreamed could happen. Just as Jesus' friends could not imagine on Friday what God would do on Sunday, we cannot now know what good, new unimaginable thing God might yet do in our lives. Easter is the ultimate sign of the enduring truth that God is never finished or through or done. That is the comfort we find in Easter's arms.

But don't get too comfortable. Don't get too comfortable in Easter's arms, because no sooner do Easter's arms take us in than they send us away. The same Easter arms that take us in and hold us near are the Easter arms that turn us around and send us out. The same Easter angel who says, "Do not be afraid," also says, "Go! Get moving. The risen Lord is already out in front of you.[3] Tell his friends to go see if they can catch up to him." That is Easter's other voice. Easter's first voice says, "Come. Come and be comforted by the fact that God has raised Jesus from death, a sure and certain sign that God is never finished or through or done." But then Easter's other voice says, "Go. Go follow the risen Christ to places you never dreamed you would go or even thought you should go." The Easter arms that embrace us and hold us also push us and send us. The Risen Lord is always out in front of us, leading us further than we meant to go, dreamed to go, or wanted to go; calling us down strange streets in unfamiliar neighbor-hoods, introducing us to people we did not plan to know, and involving us in needs we did not plan to meet.

That's the way it is with Easter. She takes us in to hold us near, but then she turns us around to send us out in the direction of the Risen Lord. And what we discover when we go where Easter sends us is that out there, stumbling off after the Risen Lord, is where the joy is! When Easter draws us near to take us in, we find hope and healing. That's where the comfort is: in Easter's arms. But the joy is in going where Easter points us when she turns us around and sends us out to try to catch up to the Risen Lord who is ever on the move. The com-fort we need is in Easter's embrace, but the joy we seek is somewhere outside our own comfort.

That's pretty much the way it is in Easter's arms. Easter opens her arms to embrace whoever is most afraid, most ashamed, most weary, sad, frustrated, bitter, embarrassed, and defeated. Easter opens her arms to hold us near and to remind us that God is never finished, through, or done with anyone. Easter embraces us in the truth that God always has something more, something good, something new that God will yet do. But the same Easter arms that hold us near also send us out, because God, who always has something new to do for us, also always has something new for us to do.

That's the way it is in Easter's arms: she pulls us in to hold us close and then spins us around to send us out. (If Easter wasn't such a good Baptist, you'd almost think she was trying to teach us to dance!)

Amen.

NOTES

[1] This was reported to me during my seminary days. I have not been able to find it in print.

[2] A saying original with the late Carlyle Marney.

[3] For the image of the risen Lord "in front of us," I am indebted to William Willimon, *The Intrusive Word* (Grand Rapids: Eerdman, 1994), 142.

CHAPTER 8

$\mathscr{A}$ $\mathscr{L}ittle$ $\mathscr{E}aster$ $\mathscr{F}ootnote$

¹When the sabbath was over, Mary Magdalene, and Mary the mother of James, and Salome bought spices, so that they might go and anoint him. ²And very early on the first day of the week, when the sun had risen, they went to the tomb. ³They had been saying to one another, "Who will roll away the stone for us from the entrance to the tomb?" ⁴When they looked up, they saw that the stone, which was very large, had already been rolled back. ⁵As they entered the tomb, they saw a young man, dressed in a white robe, sitting on the right side; and they were alarmed. ⁶But he said to them, "Do not be alarmed; you are looking for Jesus of Nazareth, who was crucified. He has been raised; he is not here. Look, there is the place they laid him. ⁷But go, tell his disciples and Peter that he is going ahead of you to Galilee; there you will see him, just as he told you." ⁸So they went out and fled from the tomb, for terror and amazement had seized them; and they said nothing to anyone, for they were afraid. (Mark 16:1-8)

Hidden away in the next-to-last verse of Mark's Easter morning report is a little Easter morning footnote. When the Easter angel sent the sunrise messengers to go tell the disciples to meet the risen Lord in Galilee, the instructions included that little footnote, "Tell Peter, too."

At first glance, it seems a bit redundant for Peter to be singled out and called by name. After all, Peter was one of the disciples, and the

Easter angel's invitation was for all the disciples. But when you think of the kind of week Peter had had, you can see why the Easter angel called Peter by name. Peter was a special case because Peter was in special pain. None of the disciples had been shining models of courage that weekend, but Peter had fallen particularly hard. The night before Jesus died, when the people around the fire asked Peter if he was a follower of Jesus, he denied that he even knew Jesus. The subject came up three times, and all three times Peter denied any connection to Jesus. Indeed, so severe was Peter's desire to distance himself from the dangers of discipleship that he punctuated his denials with oaths and curses. And to make matters worse, earlier that same evening Jesus had warned Peter that before sunrise Peter would face enormous pressure that would cause him to forsake Jesus, and Peter had responded to Jesus' warning by promising that he would never let Jesus down. Then, Peter went out and did exactly what he promised he would never do. So the last time we saw Peter, he was weeping, brokenhearted, embarrassed, and ashamed. In the light of all that, Peter might have thought his failure to stand with Jesus in Jesus' most difficult hour would make him less than welcome at the Easter meeting. Peter might have been too ashamed to show up, which is probably why, when the Easter angel said, "Go tell the disciples that the Risen Lord is waiting for them in Galilee," the Easter angel also said, "And tell Peter, too." That way Peter would know that no matter how badly he had failed, he was not finished and his life with Jesus was not over. To the contrary, Peter was welcome, wanted, and expected at the Easter meeting with the risen Lord.

Now, if you've got your life all together, if you've never been embarrassed about yourself or disappointed in yourself or ashamed of yourself, that may not mean a whole lot to you. But if, on the other hand, you have ever known the deep shame that comes with real failure, then "Tell Peter, too" may be Easter's best news for you. For some of us, the biggest Easter headline might be traveling in the smallest Easter footnote, because "Tell Peter, too" is a small Easter sign of the big Easter truth that God is never finished or done with anyone.

Easter brings us many messages, one of which is that we are dealing with a God who is never finished. When Jesus died on Friday afternoon, as far as anyone could see, it was over. His life was over. His work was over. Jesus was dead and it was over. But, much to everyone's surprise, God wasn't finished. God wasn't out of options. God had something else, something more, something new left to do. God raised Jesus from death, and the resurrection became the latest and biggest in a long line of signs that we are dealing with a God who is never finished, through, or done. The famous baseball player and linguist Yogi Berra taught us to say, "It ain't over till it's over." Easter teaches us to say, "Even when it's over, it still ain't over." The God who raised Jesus from death always has something more, something else, something new left to do this side of the grave. (And maybe even the other side of the grave. After all, where did God send Jesus once Jesus was raised from death? According to a Bible book that bears Peter's name, the risen Lord descended into hell to preach to "the spirits in prison." Well, now. What does that mean? Who can know how far this Easter God will go?)

The Easter God is never finished, through, or done with anyone. That is the truth that comes home to our lives in the tiny Easter footnote, "Tell Peter, too." The tiny Easter footnote that has Peter's name in it has our names on it. "Tell Peter, too" is a sign of something; something good and big and full of hope. It is a sign that no matter how poorly we may have chosen or how miserably we may have failed, God is not finished with us. Even if everyone who knows us has written us off as too broken, too guilty, too weak, or too wrong, God has not. It is not in God's nature to write people off or cast people away. Remember, this is the Easter God we're talking about, and the Easter God always has something else, something more, something new to do for us, and something new for us to do.

Just ask Peter. One minute, he's cussing around a campfire, swearing nine ways to Sunday that he's never met Jesus. Next thing you know, several large church buildings and two small Bible books are named after him . . . which is exactly the sort of thing we would expect from an Easter kind of God who is never finished or through or done with anyone.

Amen.

CHAPTER 9

The Nearest Thing to a Clean Slate

¹ To you, O LORD, I lift up my soul. ² O my God, in you I trust; do not let me be put to shame; do not let my enemies exult over me. ³ Do not let those who wait for you be put to shame; let them be ashamed who are wantonly treacherous. ⁴ Make me to know your ways, O LORD; teach me your paths. ⁵ Lead me in your truth, and teach me, for you are the God of my salvation; for you I wait all day long. ⁶ Be mindful of your mercy, O LORD, and of your steadfast love, for they have been from of old. ⁷ Do not remember the sins of my youth or my transgressions; according to your steadfast love remember me, for your goodness' sake, O LORD! ⁸ Good and upright is the LORD; therefore he instructs sinners in the way. ⁹ He leads the humble in what is right, and teaches the humble his way. ¹⁰ All the paths of the LORD are steadfast love and faithfulness, for those who keep his covenant and his decrees. ¹¹ For your name's sake, O LORD, pardon my guilt, for it is great. ¹² Who are they that fear the LORD? He will teach them the way that they should choose. ¹³ They will abide in prosperity, and their children shall possess the land. ¹⁴ The friendship of the LORD is for those who fear him, and he makes his covenant known to them. ¹⁵ My eyes are ever toward the LORD, for he will pluck my feet out of the net. ¹⁶ Turn to me and be gracious to me, for I am lonely and afflicted. ¹⁷ Relieve the troubles of my heart, and bring me out of my

distress. [18]Consider my affliction and my trouble, and forgive all my sins.
[19]Consider how many are my foes, and with what violent hatred they hate me.
[20]O guard my life, and deliver me; do not let me be put to shame, for I take
refuge in you. [21]May integrity and uprightness preserve me, for I wait for you.
[22]Redeem Israel, O God, out of all its troubles. (Psalm 25)

It appears that, somewhere along the way, the psalmist has acquired some "baggage." Not "baggage" as in "luggage," not "baggage" as in "Please exercise caution when opening overhead bins." Not that kind of baggage. The psalmist is carrying the other kind of baggage. You know, the kind that is even harder to put down than it is to carry. The psalmist is carrying the baggage of his past. Somewhere back there along the way he must have made a poor choice or taken a wrong path, because you have to be carrying that kind of baggage before you can pray this kind of prayer. "Do not remember the sins of my youth," the psalmist prays in verse 7. "Do not remember my transgressions." And, because guilt is never set aside as easily as that, the psalmist raises the same issue again in verse 11 when he prays, "O LORD, pardon my guilt, for it is great." And, because this kind of baggage really is even harder to put down than it is to carry, he prays again in verse 18, "God, consider my trouble and forgive my sin."

We like this psalmist a lot because this psalmist is a lot like us. He has a past, and so do we. His past is less than perfect, and so is ours. He knows the silent gnawing of his own unforgettable guilt, and so do we. He might like to have back, take back, undo or do over some word he said or choice he made, but he can't. Nor can we. Life doesn't come with a rewind button. What's done is done.

Ernest Campbell once captured "what's done is done" in a powerful bit of wisdom he gleaned from a major-league baseball locker room in the late 1980s. The California Angels were locked in a close battle for their division championship. There was less than a week left in the season. Every contest was crucial. In this particular game, the Angels had a seemingly insurmountable lead going into the final two innings, but their bullpen collapsed and they let a sure win slip away. Afterward, in the losing locker room, a sports reporter said to one of the Angels' veteran players, "This loss has dealt a crippling blow to your pennant hopes. You must be devastated." To which the player replied, "Yes, that was a terrible loss. One of the most disappointing of my career." He went on to say that the late-inning collapse was embarrassing and inexcusable. And then he said, "But that one is over, and we'll just have to stop wanting that one."[1] "That one is over, and we'll just have to stop wanting that one" rings true in the ears of those of us who have ever longed to undo or do over or take back a word, a choice, or a moment. That time we should have held our tongue, but instead spoke wounding words to someone we love? That one is over, and we'll have to stop wanting that one. That time we should have spoken the truth, but instead we fell silent because we didn't have the courage to speak up? That one is over, and we'll have to stop wanting that one. That time we said "Yes" to something we should have said "No" to? That time we said "No" when we should have said "Yes"? That time we turned away when we should have turned around? That time we didn't take the trip or spend the money or make the call that could have given joy and caused happiness and offered comfort? Those times are over, and we'll have to stop wanting them because we can't have them back.

That means no one ever gets to start over with an absolutely clean slate. If having a clean slate means all the consequences of our choices and all the results of our decisions and all the pain from our words can somehow be erased, then there are no absolutely clean slates. But the good news is that even if there are no clean slates, there are new chances. We might not be able to start over from "back there," but we can start over from "right here." The next best thing to having a clean slate behind you is having an open path before you. And that is exactly what we have . . . an open path before us. It might not be as perfect as having a clean slate, but, short of being able to start over from the beginning, which no one can do, the next best thing is starting over from here, which everyone can do.

The open path always starts out as a narrow way, narrow in the sense that we can only start down it once we are willing to speak precise and careful truth about our sin and our guilt, about the wounds we have inflicted and the wounds we have received. In one of his plays, T. S. Eliot wrote that wonderful line, "The future can only be built on the real past."² It's true. We can't move on until we have repented and done penance. At a minimum, to do penance means to speak the truth about our failures and sins and to ask forgiveness from those we have hurt or harmed. Only then are we ready to move on. The way forward is that narrow at first. But don't let that stop you. Though the way forward starts out narrow, it ends up wide, very wide, wide enough for us and all our baggage. In fact, at its widest point, the way forward is as wide as Isaiah 43:25—"Do not remember the former things, for I am about to do a new thing. I will blot out your transgressions and I will not remember your sins"—and as big as 2 Corinthians 5:17—"If anyone is in Christ they are a new creature, old things are passed away, all things are made new."

I wish we had clean slates to give out, but that would mean starting over from the beginning, which no one can do. We don't exactly have clean slates to offer, but we do have this wonderful wide-open path. It's the next best thing to a clean slate. We might not be able to start over from the beginning, but we can start over from here.

Amen.

NOTES

¹ Quoted from one of Ernest Campbell's quarterly newsletters, date unknown.

² *T. S. Eliot, The Complete Poems and Plays* (New York: Harcourt, Bruce, and Company, 1952), 228.

CHAPTER 10

Do Not Try This at Home

⁶Humble yourselves therefore under the mighty hand of God, so that he may exalt you in due time. ⁷Cast all your anxiety on him, because he cares for you. ⁸Discipline yourselves, keep alert. Like a roaring lion your adversary the devil prowls around, looking for someone to devour. ⁹Resist him, steadfast in your faith, for you know that your brothers and sisters in all the world are undergoing the same kinds of suffering. ¹⁰And after you have suffered for a little while, the God of all grace, who has called you to his eternal glory in Christ, will himself restore, support, strengthen, and establish you. ¹¹To him be the power forever and ever. Amen. (1 Peter 5:6-11)

Do not try this at home. First Peter 5:7, I mean: "Cast all your anxieties on God." Do not try it at home. That commandment is hard to keep at home alone. For casting all our cares upon God, we need help. For this, we need the church.

Even a casual reading of 1 Peter leaves no doubt that it was written to people who had cause to be anxious, worried, and afraid. Throughout the letter there are hints and clues of pressure, trouble, stress, and tension. It was a letter intended for troubled eyes, mailed to people who needed courage and strength to make it through a difficult time. And, into the midst of it all, the letter writer dropped that incredible command, "Cast all your anxiety on God, because God cares for you." I cannot imagine a more difficult commandment to keep. Some have managed to reduce the complexity of it all to simple slogans: "Let go and let God" . . . "Take your burdens to the Lord and leave them there." They make nice religious-sounding mottos, but they simply fail to take into account the enormous complexity of the gnawing shadows of anxiety, worry, and fear.

Needless to say, anxiety, worry, and fear are not necessarily indicative of a deficient faith. There are people of deep commitment and real faith who struggle all their lives with anxiety, worry, and fear. For many, anxiety has physiological causes. For some, medication is as necessary to address anxiety as it is to address diabetes or heart disease, and their anxiety is no more a commentary on their faith than a broken leg or a bad back would be.

But even for those who are not struggling with physiologically based anxiety, "casting our anxieties on God" is no simple matter. How does one do it? How does one keep that complex commandment to "cast all our anxiety on God"? I'm not so sure *one* can keep that commandment. "Cast all your anxiety on God" is so complex a commandment that most of us cannot keep it alone. By ourselves, on our own, we each are like the chorus singers in T. S. Eliot's *Murder in the Cathedral* who said, "We have all had our private terrors, our particular shadows, our secret fears . . . which no one understands."[1] That would describe most of us, at some time or another. We have our own anxieties and our own fears. We seem to remember that there is a Bible verse over near the back of the book that says, "Perfect love casts out all fear." We imagine that if we perfectly understood how perfectly God loves us, our anxiety would be cast out for us. But, so far, no such casting out has occurred. We pray about our anxieties. And sometimes it helps. We remind ourselves that much of what we fear most will never come to pass. (We recognize the truth in Frederick Buechner's observation that, for most of us, neither our fondest dreams nor our worst fears will come true.) And we remember that even when our fears have come to pass, we have lived through them. We have lived to laugh again. The worst days have passed just as quickly as the best. We know God cares for us. And yet, we still find this commandment, "Cast all your anxieties on God," too complex to keep all by ourselves.

Then we come to church. Now, one would think many people bringing their anxieties to one place would result in an enormous gathering of fear. But here is a wonder, a real miracle: Week after week, Sunday after Sunday, the sum total of all the fears of all the people is not more fear, but less. When we all come together, each with our own personal anxiety, our individual fear diminishes for as long as we are sitting with friends, singing the hymns, losing ourselves in the worship of God. Carlyle Marney once told of a conversation he had with his father in which the elder Mr. Marney said that, if he had his life to live over again, he would have a stronger faith. He said his life had been plagued with doubts, questions, and anxieties. Carlyle Marney said, "I never knew that, Dad. You always seemed so strong. How did you keep going?" To which his father replied, "Well, son, I would always be alright if I could just make it to the meeting."[2] It is so, isn't it? Something happens "in the meeting" that we cannot conjure up on our own. Everyone who comes to the meeting brings his or her own anxiety, worry, and fear, but once everyone arrives, the strangest thing happens. Everybody's individual fear joins everyone else's, and the result of all that addition is subtraction. Our anxiety becomes less consuming, less paralyzing, less dreadful. In some mystical way that is as undeniable as it is inexplicable, we draw strength simply from being in the presence of the people of God.

In one of Emily Dickinson's letters to a grieving friend, she wrote, "Don't cry, dear Mary. Let us do that for you, because you are too tired now. We don't know how dark it is, but if you are at sea, perhaps when we say we are there, you won't be as afraid. The waves are very big, but every one that covers you, covers us, too."[3] That is the kind of thing that happens in church. The people of God comfort one another and, in some mystical way that can never be fully explained, draw strength from one another.

In her book *Traveling Mercies*, Anne Lamott has a chapter called "Why I Make Sam Go to Church," in which she says she makes her son go to church because she wants him to find what she has found, "a path and a little light to see by." She then goes on to say, concerning her church, this simple, beautiful sentence: "When I was at the end of my rope, the people at St. Andrew tied a knot in it for me and helped me hold on."[4]

It happens in church. At the meeting, surrounded by the family of faith, we stand our best chance of actually keeping this complex commandment to "cast all our cares on God." Our cares, our fears, our anxieties are too heavy for us to cast on God all by ourselves. For this, we need the church. We have bowed too low for too long at the personal altar of individualism. We need one another. We need the church, the family of faith, the meeting.

When it comes to casting all your anxieties on God, do not try this at home. For this, we need the church. The church isn't perfect and it isn't magic and it doesn't fix everything all at once or once and for all. But every week we get to go back and find, once more, the strength and courage to start out all over again; strength and courage we might never have known at home alone. It happens in church.

Amen.

NOTES

[1] T. S. Eliot, *The Complete Poems and Plays* (New York: Harcourt Brace and Company, 1950), 181.

[2] I heard this story in a sermon by Welton Gaddy.

[3] *Selected Poems and Letters of Emily Dickinson*, ed. Robert N. Linscott (New York: Daubleday, 1959), 282.

[4] Anne Lamott, *Traveling Mercies* (New York: Pantheon Books, 1999), 100.

CHAPTER 11

Will the Cycle Be Unbroken?

²⁷The days are surely coming, says the LORD, when I will sow the house of Israel and the house of Judah with the seed of humans and the seed of animals. ²⁸And just as I have watched over them to pluck up and break down, to overthrow, destroy, and bring evil, so I will watch over them to build and to plant, says the LORD. ²⁹In those days they shall no longer say: "The parents have eaten sour grapes, and the children's teeth are set on edge." ³⁰But all shall die for their own sins; the teeth of everyone who eats sour grapes shall be set on edge. (Jeremiah 31:27-30)

When that doctor asked me,
"Son how'd you get in this condition?"
I said, "Hey Sawbones, I'm just carrying on
An old family tradition."[1]

With those words, the famous twentieth-century American poet Hank Williams Jr. put a frame around the truth that travels in that odd sentence in Jeremiah 31:29, "The parents have eaten sour grapes, and the children's teeth are set on edge." This was an old saying that circulated among the Hebrew people; a popular proverb about family ties, sort of like "The apple doesn't fall far from the tree" or "Like father like son" or "The gene pool could use a little chlorine" or "I'm becoming my mother." "The parents ate sour grapes, and the children's teeth were set on edge" is just another way of saying what everybody already knows, which is that our lives are tied to, and colored by, our family of origin.

In my family, for example, we have what I call the "Gene Poole gene pool." Every family has a gene pool, but we're the only family I know that has a gene pool named Gene Poole. Gene Poole was my grandfather. We called him Daddy Gene. Daddy Gene is my all-time favorite ancestor, but he died when I was eight, so most of what I know about him I know from the stories, of which there were many. All the stories had a common theme that I am sure had become embellished and exaggerated as the years had passed, but all of them essentially boiled down to this: Daddy Gene was a natural-born comedian/entertainer/piano player who frequently found it difficult to harvest a crop because he couldn't quit playing long enough to work. That is the essential sum of the many amusing Gene Poole stories. But for my dad, who was a teenager during the depths of the depression, it wasn't so funny at the time, because Daddy Gene's less than stellar work ethic meant that, in a time when everyone was poor, the Pooles were among the poorest. So what did my father do? He turned in the exact opposite direction. (The parents ate sour grapes, and the children's teeth were set on edge.) He worked all the time; repairing refrigerators, rebuilding air conditioners, plowing vegetable gardens, collecting metal to sell at the junkyard, and rousing me from bed early on Saturday mornings to make sure I didn't grow up to be lazy; hammering into me the idea that I had to constantly be working to "make something out of myself." But every now and then, no matter how hard he worked to suppress it, the Gene Poole part of our gene pool would surface in my dad, usually on Saturday nights during the Lawrence Welk Show or the Hayloft Jamboree. As for me, I worked and worked to "make something of myself," but the Gene Poole gene pool kept getting me in trouble for doing Elvis impersonations in the lunch line at Central High School in Macon, Georgia. And a few years ago when I saw Josh and Maria take over the dance floor at a wedding reception, I thought to myself, "The gene pool is strong, especially the Gene Poole part."

I offer that from my own life as a simple embodiment of the perpetual truth that, for better or worse, for good or bad, one generation shapes and colors the next. "The parents ate sour grapes and the children's teeth were set on edge," or "The parents ate sweet grapes and the children's teeth were set to singing." Either way, for good or bad and usually for both, each generation is shaped and colored by the last generation.

Though it is so that there is an undeniable link between the generations, we have to be careful how we say it, lest we start using family history to excuse ourselves from personal responsibility for our own lives. Apparently, that is what was happening with the Hebrews, which is why Jeremiah said, "It's time to stop saying 'The parents ate sour grapes, and the children's teeth were set on edge.'" Apparently, people had started using that as an excuse. In other words, *I can't help being the way I am. I'm paying for my parents' sins. After all, you know what they say—"The parents ate bitter grapes and the children's teeth were set on edge."* Apparently, God got tired of that. In fact, over in Ezekiel 18:1-3, we read these words: "Thus says the LORD, why do you keep repeating this proverb, 'The parents ate bitter grapes and the children's teeth were set on edge.' This proverb shall no more be used by you . . . . It is only the person who sins who will pay for that sin." God wants people to take responsibility for their own lives and stop blaming their problems on past generations. "Stop saying that thing about the parents ate bitter grapes," says God, "and start taking responsibility for your own actions. No scapegoats. No blame game. Own your own guilt, and change your own ways."

God's word to them is a good word for us. If there are destructive cycles in our family history, we can take responsibility for breaking those cycles by deciding to speak and act in a new way. If, for example, a person comes from a home where people were managed and controlled by withheld blessings and subtle messages of disapproval, if they continue that cycle, they don't get to excuse themselves by saying, "Well, that's how I was raised." Rather, they have to name that cycle as sinful and choose to speak and act in new ways that give grace and unconditional blessing to others.

This is not simple or easy. It doesn't happen all at once. It is complex work that can take a lifetime of practice. We will need help to break those old cycles, and even then we never get it all perfectly right. Our parents weren't perfect, and neither were theirs. We who are parents now aren't perfect, and our children won't be perfect parents to their children. It always has been and always will be true, for every generation, that "The parents ate bitter grapes and the children had a bad taste." But it is also true that we can choose to break old cycles. We can decide to speak and act in new ways.

The poet George Eliot once said, "It is never too late to become the person you might have been."[2] It's true. It may be too late for some things to be fixed or undone or redone. That's the sad truth we have to face. But we must also embrace the glad truth that it is never too late to break that old "bitter grapes-to-edgy-teeth" cycle by taking responsibility for our own lives and deciding, with God's help and the help of God's people, actually to change.

It is never too late to become the person you might have been. On the other hand, it is never too early, either.

Amen.

NOTES

[1] Written and performed by Hank Williams Jr., "Family Tradition" appears on the Hank Williams Jr. Greatest Hits collection (Nashville: Curb Music, 1993).

[2] As quoted in Edward Cohen, *The Peddler's Grandson* (Jackson: University Press of Mississippi, 1999), 25. The original sentence, "It is never too late to be what you might have been," is slightly altered here.

CHAPTER 12

Unfinished Business

³³The king was deeply moved, and went up to the chamber over the gate, and wept; and as he went, he said, "O my son Absalom, my son, my son Absalom! Would I had died instead of you, O Absalom, my son, my son!" (2 Samuel 18:33)

I'm sure there must be sadder sentences somewhere, but not many much sadder than David's lament at Absalom's death: "Absalom, Absalom, my son Absalom. Would that I had died instead of you."

There's a lot of life compressed into that single sorrowful sentence. It wraps a dark frame around a family portrait full of conflict, struggle, and pain. Absalom and his father David are, like many Old Testament families, a study in complex and conflicted relationships. Absalom had launched an effort to usurp his father's throne, an effort that began as a covert operation but reached a violent conclusion when Absalom fought his final battle against his father David. Second Samuel 18:5 says David asked the commanders of his army to go easy on Absalom, to defeat Absalom's army but to spare Absalom's life. But, despite David's pleas, Absalom did not survive the battle. Second Samuel 18:9 says that, in the midst of the combat, Absalom's hair became entangled in a low-hanging tree branch. His horse kept going, leaving Absalom out on a limb, so to speak. King David's soldiers found him in that defenseless predicament and proceeded to kill him, which led to David's sad saying, "Absalom, Absalom. My son Absalom, would that I had died instead of you." And with that, David and Absalom became a most extreme example of that old cliché about "unfinished business."

Most of us will never experience the depth of unfinished business that David and Absalom knew because we don't have the kind of family conflict that results in all-out war. And yet, most of us have at least a little of what David and Absalom had a lot of. We live with a certain amount of unfinished business, which sometimes leaves us, like David, trying to tell someone something after they're already gone.

I guess that's why some of us talk to graves. Whenever we go home to Georgia, I usually slip away at some point and go to my father's grave. I always start out pulling the weeds and straightening the flowers, but I always end up talking to his grave. I know he's not "there," but still I always end up talking to him. It's a much less interesting version of David talking to Absalom after it was too late for Absalom to hear what David wanted to say. It's just a typical, ordinary effort at taking care of unfinished business.

On the one hand, of course, you could call such efforts pointless, futile, and meaningless. After all, the person with whom you had unfinished business is gone. They can't hear you apologize or forgive. And anyway, it's over. I suppose that's one way to look at our unfinished business with family members who have died. But the other side of the truth is that even if they're gone, you're not. You're still here living with whatever was unspoken, unresolved, and unfinished. So don't be too quick to dismiss the idea of working on unfinished business with loved ones who have died. In fact, sometimes, *after* the funeral may be the only time the conversation can ever take place because the fear of resolving the unfinished business with your living loved one is just too paralyzing. You know you ought to do it, but you can't. So you never do. And then one day you find yourself talking to a grave. And it helps a little. It's not magic, but at least the unfinished business sometimes seems a little less unfinished when you talk about it, even if you're talking to a grave.

Of course, under ideal circumstances we don't have to worry about all that. Under ideal circumstances, we stay so caught up with our family members that even if their death is as sudden for us as Absalom's was for David, there is no unfinished anything; no unspoken apology, no unforgiven wrong, no unexpressed gratitude. That, of course, would be the best. Some folks live that way. But some don't, and we're the ones who end up like David talking to Absalom, talking to people after they're gone.

I'm sure David thought there would be another chance for him to be reconciled to Absalom. Instead, all he could do was talk to his grave. So let us all take a lesson about our unfinished business from David and Absalom's unfinished business. There may be unfinished business we can't bring up because the risks outweigh the hopes, but to the extent that we can, we should write the letters, make the calls, and have the conversations that confront the wrongs, forgive the wounds, confess the sins, tell the love, and express the gratitude that, left unspoken, simply end up as unfinished business in a cemetery someday. As Fredrich Schleirmacher said when he preached the sermon for his son's funeral, "Let us all love one another as persons who can soon—alas, how soon!—be snatched away."[1]

But what if it's already too late? What if you didn't stay caught up, leaving you to live with unfinished business that is now too late to be resolved? If that is your case, then always remember this: Revelation 21:25. That's the verse in the back of the Bible that says the gates of pearl are never closed. Revelation 21:25 says God is holding twelve gates open, never to be closed. Perhaps that is a sign of something. Perhaps it is a sign of the fact that, with God, it's never too late. Perhaps even our most unfinished business, which seems so final at the grave, is not beyond being resolved. Perhaps the gates are open still for forgiveness and peace. Perhaps even David and Absalom were finally all right. I choose to believe they are. In a letter to Mary Bowles, Emily Dickinson once wrote, "David's grieved decision haunted me when a little girl. I hope he has found Absalom."[2] I hope so, too. I have no chapter or verse to support such a notion, but I do choose to believe that even David and Absalom have found one another and that, somehow, they are finally all right.

I choose to believe we will be too, because I really do believe all those gates that won't close are signs of an open future where God will take all that has somehow gone wrong and somehow make it right.

Amen.

NOTES

[1] From "Sermon at Nathaneal's Grave," *A Chorus of Witnesses*, ed. Thomas G. Long and Cornelius Platinga Jr. (Grand Rapids: Eerdmans, 1994), 261.

[2] *Selected Poems and Letters of Emily Dickinson*, ed. Robert N. Linscott (New York: Doubleday, 1959), 314.

CHAPTER 13

Who's In? Who's Out?

²⁴ He put before them another parable: "The kingdom of heaven may be compared to someone who sowed good seed in his field; ²⁵ but while everybody was asleep, an enemy came and sowed weeds among the wheat, and then went away. ²⁶ So when the plants came up and bore grain, then the weeds appeared as well. ²⁷ And the slaves of the householder came and said to him, 'Master, did you not sow good seed in your field? Where, then, did these weeds come from?' ²⁸ He answered, 'An enemy has done this.' The slaves said to him, 'Then do you want us to go and gather them?' ²⁹ But he replied, 'No; for in gathering the weeds you would uproot the wheat along with them. ³⁰ Let both of them grow together until the harvest; and at harvest time I will tell the reapers, Collect the weeds first and bind them in bundles to be burned, but gather the wheat into my barn.'" . . . ³⁶ Then he left the crowds and went into the house. And his disciples approached him, saying, "Explain to us the parable of the weeds of the field." ³⁷ He answered, "The one who sows the good seed is the Son of Man; ³⁸ the field is the world, and the good seed are the children of the kingdom; the weeds are the children of the evil one, ³⁹ and the enemy who sowed them is the devil; the harvest is the end of the age, and the reapers are angels. ⁴⁰ Just as the weeds are collected and burned up with fire, so will it be at the end of the age. ⁴¹ The Son of Man will send his angels, and they will collect out of his kingdom all causes of sin and all evildoers, ⁴² and they will throw them into the furnace

*of fire, where there will be weeping and gnashing of teeth. *[43]*Then the righteous will shine like the sun in the kingdom of their Father. Let anyone with ears listen!" (Matthew 13:24-30, 36-43)*

There seems to be a pattern in the Gospels; a sort of "Who's in? Who's out?" pattern. The pattern winds its way along a path that goes something like this: In Matthew 9:10-12, religious leaders who assume they are securely inside God's family assail Jesus for breaking bread with sinners, whom they assume to be outside God's family. In Matthew 20:1-16, Jesus tells a parable in which last-minute workers, representative of all outsiders, turn out to be as inside the kingdom as the all-day workers. In Matthew 21:31, Jesus declares that the tax collectors and prostitutes, his society's leading religious outsiders, would enter the kingdom of God ahead of the Pharisees, his society's leading religious insiders. The pattern continues in Mark 2:15, where Jesus welcomes several sinful outsiders, prompting complaints from religious insiders. In Mark 9:38-39, John stops a stranger from casting out a demon in Jesus' name because the stranger is not inside Jesus' group, but Jesus reprimands John with a memorable sentence that brings outsiders inside when he says, "Whoever is not against us is for us." In Luke 7:39, a Pharisee who is confident that he is in God's tight circle is indignant because Jesus embraces a visitor who is well known to be outside of God's family. In Luke 15, those who are on the inside complain some more about Jesus' indiscriminate welcome of outsiders, which prompts Jesus to tell his most famous story, the parable of the prodigal son. In Luke 18:9-14, it is the tax collector (who is assumed to be on the outside of God) who goes home right with God, not the religious leader (who is assumed to be on the inside with God.) And, finally, in John 10:16, Jesus says enough to keep everyone a little off balance from now on when it comes to who's in with God and who's out: "I have other sheep that do not belong to this fold."[1] Who are those "other sheep"? Only Jesus knows who he had in mind when he said he has "other sheep that don't belong to this fold."

That seems to be the point of the "Who's in? Who's out?" pattern winding its way through the Gospels. The point is, we don't know who's in and who's out. God knows, but we don't. That's also the point of the parable about the weeds and wheat. The parable Jesus told in Matthew 13 is a speed bump to slow the haste of those who would be too sure about too much too soon when it comes to who's in God's kingdom and who's out. The workers in the parable are ready and willing to pull up the weeds growing among the wheat. "Do you want us to go and pull out the weeds?" they ask. But the landowner tells them to leave it alone. It's not their job. "No, for in gathering the weeds you would uproot the wheat along with them. Let both of them grow together until the harvest." The point of the parable is that making judgments about who does and does not belong in God's family is work that is not ours to do. That work, the work of ultimate judgment, is beyond us. We don't know enough to get that right. That's the point of the parable, which fits the pattern of all those other Gospel passages. Throughout the four Gospels, Jesus consistently declines all offers from would-be theological bodyguards, no matter how sincere or well intentioned they might be. Jesus consistently refuses to endorse the conventional wisdom about "who's in" and "who's out," which should be warning enough to keep us careful about judgment, lest we speak with too much clarity and too little charity concerning who is in God's kingdom and who is out.

On the other hand, we also must be careful not to lapse into a nonchalant, lackadaisical "anything-goes" approach to right and wrong, truth and falsehood. The fact is, there are judgments that must be made. It would be nice if we could all retreat into the tolerant shade of Matthew 7:1 ("Do not judge, so that you may not be judged."). But the same Bible that gives us Matthew 7:1 also gives us (on the same page!) Matthew 7:15-16, "Beware of false prophets . . . . You will know them by their fruits." Obviously, the same Jesus who said "Judge not" expects us to make some judgments. Then there is Paul, who said in Romans 14:13, "Let us therefore no longer pass judgment on one another," but who indicted the church at Corinth for failing to pass judgment on the immoral behavior of one of their members (1 Corinthians 5:1-11).

So, which is it? Should we judge or should we not? The answer, apparently, is "Yes." We must make judgments about right and wrong, good and evil. Without such judgments, the church would never confront injustice, violence, racism, or any number of other wrongs that must be confronted in our world. But when it comes to the ultimate judgment between "Who's in?" and "Who's out?" that's the point at which the parable of the weeds and the wheat causes us to lose our voices and fall silent in the face of mystery.

Early one May morning, I was walking alone in the Frio River canyon, home of Laity Lodge Retreat Center in the hill country of Texas. As the sun rose, I heard, from high in the river bluffs, the bleating of a mountain goat or a lost sheep. Once I returned to the retreat center, I asked some of the canyon's veteran residents if there were sheep or goats living in the canyons. "Both," was their reply. "There are wild Spanish goats in these hills and stray mountain sheep as well." "Which do you think I was hearing this morning, crying in the canyon?" I asked. "No way to know," they said. "They sound so much alike you can't tell the sheep from the goats."

No way to know, indeed. We don't know enough to tell the sheep from the goats. Or the weeds from the wheat. Who are the sheep? Who are the goats? Who is the wheat? Who are the weeds? Who's in? Who's out? Such judgment is God's work, not ours. The best and the most we can say about ultimate, final, eternal judgment may be to borrow that beautiful line from Frederick Buechner: "The One who is going to judge us most finally is the same one who has always loved us most fully."[2]

That is very good news for all of us because, let's face it, not only do the weeds and the wheat both grow together around us, they also both grow together within us.[3]

Amen.

NOTES

[1] For this way of thinking about John 10:16, I am indebted to William Willimon, *The Intrusive Word* (Grand Rapids: Eerdmans, 1994), 84.

[1] Frederick Buechner, *Listening to Your Life* (New York: Harper Collins, 1992), 58.

[2] The idea that the weeds and the wheat grow together within us was spawned for me by David Buttrick, *Speaking Parables* (Louisville: Westminster John Knox Press, 2000), 93-98.

CHAPTER 14

Go and Learn What this Means

⁹As Jesus was walking along, he saw a man called Matthew sitting at the tax booth; and he said to him, "Follow me." And he got up and followed him. ¹⁰And as he sat at dinner in the house, many tax collectors and sinners came and were sitting with him and his disciples. ¹¹When the Pharisees saw this, they said to his disciples, "Why does your teacher eat with tax collectors and sinners?" ¹²But when he heard this, he said, "Those who are well have no need of a physician, but those who are sick. ¹³Go and learn what this means, 'I desire mercy, not sacrifice.' For I have come to call not the righteous but sinners." (Matthew 9:9-13)

"Who's in? Who's out?" is not the only pattern that weaves its way through the Gospels. Another pattern emerges here and there, showing up often enough to be discernable even to the most casual eye. The pattern first appears in Mark 2, where, instead of rejoicing to see Jesus eating with sinners, Jesus' critics are distressed that he is enjoying table fellowship that colors outside the lines of their religious traditions. In Mark 3, it happens again: Instead of rejoicing to see Jesus heal the man with the withered hand, Jesus' critics are angry because the healing occurred on the Sabbath, thus violating another religious tradition. In Luke 7, instead of rejoicing to see Jesus' friendship with a known sinner, they are dismayed that he accepts her gestures of love because his behavior goes against their long-held convictions. In Luke 13, Jesus' critics are indignant because Jesus heals a woman on the Sabbath. In Luke 15, they are scandalized by Jesus' welcome of outcasts and sinners. In John 5, they are furious with Jesus for healing the lame man at Bethsaida on a Sabbath, and in John 9 Jesus' critics are in an uproar because Jesus has opened the eyes of a blind man on the Sabbath. Over and over it happens in the Gospels: Jesus' most scrupulously religious observers cannot rejoice over the right things because they are too worried about the wrong things.

Such, of course, is the case in Matthew 9, another passage in the pattern. The occasion is another one of Jesus' many dinners with sinners. Verses 10 and 11 tell the story: "As Jesus sat at dinner in the house, many tax collectors and sinners came and were sitting with Jesus and the disciples. When the Pharisees saw this they said to the disciples, 'Why does your teacher eat with tax collectors and sinners?'" In verse 12, Jesus overhears the complaint cloaked in a question, and in verse 13 he sends his critics back to Sunday school with a simple assignment: "Go and learn what this means: 'I desire mercy and not sacrifice.'"

When Jesus responds to his critics with those instructions, he is sending them back to the Hebrew Bible, of course; back to Hosea 6:6. When we find those words, "I desire mercy and not sacrifice," in Hosea 6:6, God's people have lost their way. They still have their worship services and they still offer sacrifices, but their lives don't reflect the character of God. There is a tragic absence of commitment to the central, core values of justice and mercy that God has called God's people to embody. So when God, through the prophet Hosea, is trying to call the people back into a life of genuine worship and authentic service, one of the things God says to them is "I desire steadfast love, not sacrifice." God says that what God really cares about is not how scrupulously God's people can maintain the rules and regulations of their religious system. Rather, what God really longs to see in

God's people is steadfast love; lives compelled, governed, and motivated by mercy.

In Matthew 9:13, Jesus invokes those words from Hosea 6:6 to help people who have missed the point find their way back to what matters most. The people to whom Jesus says, "Go and learn what this means, 'I desire mercy and not sacrifice,'" are not bad people. They are, to the contrary, very good people. They are perhaps among the most meticulously religious people Jesus knows. Their problem is that they have lost sight of what really matters. They don't get it. They've missed the point. What they are worried about is a clear symptom of what they don't understand. The fact that they are bothered by Jesus sharing a table with sinners is a clear symptom of the fact they have lost sight of the truth that God loves those sinners and God wants to embrace them and receive them and welcome them. If these nice people understood that, they would be rejoicing instead of fretting . . . they would be pleased, not angered. They are worrying about protecting their traditions when they should be rejoicing over what Jesus is doing. Their lives are driven by the fear that what they have always thought might be set aside, because they've always been taught that you don't embrace and welcome certain kinds of sinners. Their lives are driven by fear rather than by love.

So Jesus says, "You all need to go learn what God meant when God said, 'I desire mercy and not sacrifice.' What you're worried about doesn't matter when placed alongside a world filled with great need, deep pain, and real opportunities to help the hurting and embrace the lonely and show mercy and grace to those who have been broken by life's hardest twists and turns."

That's what Jesus says to them. And us. We have to go learn what this means. Imagine the people we might have been if early on we had learned what "God desires mercy, not sacrifice" means and had then lived with no other agenda than to embody the mercy God desires. What sort of people would we be if our only agenda was to embody God's kind of steadfast love and mercy? It isn't too late. It is not yet too late for us to go learn what this means. But neither is it too soon, so we should probably go now. We should go and learn what this means: "God desires mercy, not sacrifice."

Do not die before you learn what this means, because to die without learning what this means would be to miss the best part of who you might have been. It won't keep you out of heaven, if you die without knowing what this means. You won't miss out on the next life. It's just this life that you'll miss . . . the life you could have known . . . the person you might have been, if only you had learned what this means and then lived by it.

Amen.

CHAPTER 15

A Modest Proposal for Daily Prayer

⁹He also told this parable to some who trusted in themselves that they were righteous and regarded others with contempt: ¹⁰"Two men went up to the temple to pray, one a Pharisee and the other a tax collector. ¹¹The Pharisee, standing by himself, was praying thus, 'God, I thank you that I am not like other people: thieves, rogues, adulterers, or even like this tax collector. ¹²I fast twice a week; I give a tenth of all my income.' ¹³But the tax collector, standing far off, would not even look up to heaven, but was beating his breast and saying, 'God, be merciful to me, a sinner!' ¹⁴I tell you, this man went down to his home justified rather than the other; for all who exalt themselves will be humbled, but all who humble themselves will be exalted." (Luke 18:9-14)

In addition to those other Gospel patterns, there also seems to be a pattern running through the parables. The parable pattern seems to be that the best people in the story always get the worst end of the story. Take, for example, this parable about the Pharisee and the tax collector. The Pharisee in the parable is prayerful, faithful, and moral. The Pharisee is living a disciplined life, trying to do the right thing, striving to be an honorable person, but he is the one the parable sends home unjustified. And that's not the only time something like that happens. Take the parable of the prodigal son, for instance. The prodigal son makes poor choices and wasteful decisions. He comes home broke and broken, with no one to blame but himself. His older brother, on the other hand, has stayed home and kept his shoulder to the wheel. Yet it is he, the hard-working, dependable older brother, who gets the worst end of the parable because he refuses to strap on a party hat and drink a toast to his brother's return. And don't even get me started on the parable of the all-day workers! Talk about the wrong people getting the short end of a parable! You remember that story. The farmer has a crop to harvest so he hires laborers; some at six, some at nine, some at noon, some at three, and some at five in the afternoon. At quitting time, he starts handing out the pay, and everybody gets the same. The laborers who worked one hour get exactly the same as the laborers who worked twelve hours. So, of course, the all-day workers complain. Who wouldn't? They had given the most effort, invested the most energy, and done the most labor. Yet, they're the ones who got reprimanded by the landowner: "Are you jealous because I'm generous? Can I not be as good as I wish to whomever I wish? I gave you exactly what I promised you. If I choose to give the same to these others, that's my business, not yours. Now take your money and go." Once again, the ones who have tried the hardest get the worst end of the story

There seems to be a pattern here, and it is, frankly, a little troubling. What makes the pattern troubling is the fact that the people in the parables who go away mad or unhappy happen to be the people who are most like us. We earn our keep, we like to say, so it is the all-day workers with whom folks like us most closely identify. And many of us have more in common with the older brother than the prodigal son because we are loyal and dependable and earn what we have by hard work. And most of us are closer kin to the Pharisee in today's parable than we are to the tax collector. It's troubling to admit, but the people in the parables who come off most poorly are most often us. We are the all-day workers, the elder brother, the Pharisee.

The pattern in the parables suggests that we have something to learn. What we have to learn is that when it comes to our relationship with God, we, who love to be proud of what we have earned, can earn nothing. People who think they've earned God's mercy and favor and acceptance are just as wrong as they can be. It's all gift, and the only people who go home happy and joyful and justified are those who can accept the fact that they have actually received something they did not, and cannot, earn or deserve. If we don't like that, it might be because we enjoy saying what the Pharisee said: "God, thank you that I'm not like those other people." Once we admit that we and they are all the children of grace, then we can't say that anymore. Then all we can say is "God be merciful to me, a sinner."

Every now and then, we all need to be reminded that, despite our impressive appearances, all any of us really can say is, "God be merciful to me, a sinner," because we are all the children of God's grace—loved by God, not because we are so good, but because God is so good. In fact, here is a modest proposal that might help. Try repeating this phrase several times a day every day: "God, be merciful to me, a sinner." A couple of years ago, I started making "God, be merciful to me, a sinner" a part of my daily prayers. Specifically, I write that sentence in my prayer journal almost every day. Once I started praying "God, be merciful to me, a sinner" each day and all through the day, I made a small but significant discovery. I discovered that I cannot say, "God be merciful to me, a sinner" and "Lord, I'm glad I'm not like those other folks" at the same time.

You can say one or the other, but you cannot say both.

Amen.

CHAPTER 16

Which Christ Is King?

33 When they came to the place that is called The Skull, they crucified Jesus there with the criminals, one on his right and one on his left. 34 Then Jesus said, "Father, forgive them; for they do not know what they are doing." And they cast lots to divide his clothing. 35 And the people stood by, watching; but the leaders scoffed at him, saying, "He saved others; let him save himself if he is the Messiah of God, his chosen one!" 36 The soldiers also mocked him, coming up and offering him sour wine, 37 and saying, "If you are the King of the Jews, save yourself!" 38 There was also an inscription over him, "This is the King of the Jews." 39 One of the criminals who were hanged there kept deriding him and saying, "Are you not the Messiah? Save yourself and us!" 40 But the other rebuked him, saying, "Do you not fear God, since you are under the same sentence of condemnation? 41 And we indeed have been condemned justly, for we are getting what we deserve for our deeds, but this man has done nothing wrong." 42 Then he said, "Jesus, remember me when you come into your kingdom." 43 He replied, "Truly I tell you, today you will be with me in Paradise." (Luke 23:33-43)

"Christ the King" has become, for me, a day to love and a day to fear. I love Christ the King Sunday because it always brings the Christian year to such a grand conclusion. (Plus it is always the Sunday before

Advent begins, making this the Sunday when Christmas is just the right distance away; not too far, but not too near.)

I love Christ the King Sunday, but I fear it, too. I fear it because it inevitably confronts us with the question of how we should live if Christ is, in fact, our king. Of course, that raises another hard question, which is, "Which Christ?" "Which Christ is king?" Is Christ the King the Jesus of the four Gospels, the one who had nowhere to lay his head and called his followers to a life of uncluttered simplicity, or is Christ the King the Christ of the subsequent centuries, the Christ who became the object of magnificent adornments and the subject of official doctrines and the recipient of massive properties?

It isn't easy to know what to say about all this. My own overly simplistic tendency is to say that Christ the King who rules our lives should be the Jesus of the four Gospels, which leads to the predictable conclusion that, since the church is in the world to embody the spirit of Jesus, then the church needs to read the four Gospels, live by them, and let the Jesus of the Gospels be Christ the King who rules the church. If one follows that path, then one will probably conclude that groups such as the Mennonites and the Quakers have landed nearest to Christ the King, because they more nearly embody the simple Jesus of the Gospels.

The "Christ of the centuries" view of Christ the King will take one in a different direction. The Christ of the centuries became a wealthy, powerful landowner once Constantine made Christianity a state-endorsed national religion in the fourth century. At that time, the Jesus of the Gospels, who called for a simple, uncluttered, cross-bearing kind of life, became the Christ of the centuries who was honored with lavish displays and defined by orthodox creeds. If Christ the King is the Christ of the centuries, then the church has a different yardstick by which to measure its decisions and shape its life than the simple Jesus of the four Gospels.

So, which Christ is King? The Jesus of the four Gospels or the Christ of the subsequent centuries? The Jesus of the Gospels was a Jew who came to reveal the truth about God. He never acquired material possessions. He never suggested that he intended to start a new world religion called Christianity. He called his followers to unclutter their lives and find their joy, not in prosperity or prominence or power, but in knowing God and loving people and speaking truth and doing good. He chose speaking the truth over safety and security, and he maintained his commitment to the truth even when it became clear that his commitment was going to get him killed, which it did. And then, God raised him from death. Empowered by the Holy Spirit, his followers began to proclaim what Jesus had taught them before his death. They did not start out as Christians proclaiming Christianity. They were Jews who had chosen to follow Jesus, their fellow Jew who had been born into Judaism and who had practiced Judaism all his life, keeping Passover on the night before his death. But, eventually, things changed. The followers of Jesus began to be called Christians, and what they believed began to be called Christianity. Then, with the aforementioned conversion of Constantine in the fourth century, Christianity became a national religion. Cathedrals were built in honor of one who called his followers to give up their possessions and simplify their material lives. Before long, people were going off to war in the name of one who called his followers to turn the other cheek and love their enemies, and church councils were being convened to construct official creeds in defense of one who called people to embrace not a set of doctrines but a way of life. Thus, there emerged what most people now consider to be "mainline Christianity," what I call "the Christ of the centuries."

So . . . which Christ is King? The simple Jesus of the four Gospels or the elaborate Christ of the subsequent centuries? Needless to say, it isn't as simple as that. This can be a complex question with which to struggle. I once felt the full weight of its complexity while visiting a great cathedral in New York City. In that stunningly beautiful sanctuary, I felt unusually near to God. I loved being there. The beauty of that sacred place lifted my life. But as I walked out those massive doors back onto the street, I found myself wondering, "What would Jesus say about all this?" Would Jesus say, "Thank you for honoring me by creating this beautiful place for my glory," or would Jesus say, "Which of my words in the four Gospels caused you to think I would ever want my followers to evolve into an institution with this many possessions and this much wealth?" How we answer that depends on how we answer the "Which Christ is King?" question. If our King is the Jesus of the Gospels, then perhaps he would not rejoice over his vast holdings. If our King is the Christ of the centuries, then perhaps he would.

Of course, there is always the possibility that I'm asking the wrong question. Perhaps the Jesus of the Gospels *is* the Christ of the centuries. After all, the Jesus of the Gospels did say in John 16, "I have more things to tell you now, but you cannot bear them. When the Holy Spirit comes, he will guide you into all truth." Perhaps the Christianity that has evolved into a huge institution with massive holdings and many doctrines is what Jesus would have described had he not run out of time. Maybe that's what he meant in John 16 when he said, "I have more to tell you, but not now." That would certainly take the pressure off and make things easier. Then we could declare ourselves followers of the Jesus of the four Gospels *and* the Christ of subsequent centuries. Maybe that's the answer. Maybe Christ the King is not "either/or" but "both/and."

I don't know. I don't have the answer. All I have is the question. (It is impossible to read the four Gospels and not, at least, have the question.)

Amen.

CHAPTER 17

Joseph Chose the Dream

18 Now the birth of Jesus the Messiah took place in this way. When his mother Mary had been engaged to Joseph, but before they lived together, she was found to be with child from the Holy Spirit. 19 Her husband Joseph, being a righteous man and unwilling to expose her to public disgrace, planned to dismiss her quietly. 20 But just when he had resolved to do this, an angel of the Lord appeared to him in a dream and said, "Joseph, son of David, do not be afraid to take Mary as your wife, for the child conceived in her is from the Holy Spirit. 21 She will bear a son, and you are to name him Jesus, for he will save his people from their sins." 22 All this took place to fulfill what had been spoken by the Lord through the prophet: 23 "Look, the virgin shall conceive and bear a son, and they shall name him Emmanuel," which means, "God is with us." 24 When Joseph awoke from sleep, he did as the angel of the Lord commanded him; he took her as his wife, 25 but had no marital relations with her until she had borne a son; and he named him Jesus. (Matthew 1:18-25)

Poor Joseph. What should he do? Should he follow his logical plan, or should he obey his radical dream? That is the choice Joseph must make in Matthew 1.

You will remember, of course, from Christmases past, that Joseph's fiancée is expecting a baby. Joseph does not know who the father is, but he knows who the father is not. So what is Joseph to do? Matthew is careful to say that Joseph is a righteous man, so one assumes that Joseph, a righteous Jew, is acquainted with what the Torah says. The Torah says, in Deuteronomy 22, that an engaged woman who is not faithful to her fiancé is to be stoned to death. So Joseph's first decision is a biblical interpretation matter. He decides he will not do exactly what the Bible says. He settles on a gentler way to respond than the Bible allows. His plan is described in verse 19 of Matthew 1: "Unwilling to expose Mary to public disgrace, Joseph planned to dismiss her quietly." That is Joseph's plan in verse 19. And it holds up nicely, until verse 20.

In verse 20, Joseph doses off for a moment, and while he sleeps, he dreams, and the dream he dreams in verse 20 does not exactly fit with the plan he planned in verse 19. Verse 20 says, "Just when Joseph had resolved to dismiss Mary quietly, an angel of the Lord appeared to him in a dream and said, 'Joseph, son of David, do not be afraid to take Mary as your wife; for the child conceived in her is of the Holy Spirit.'" Now, a little deeper down the page, in verse 24, Matthew says, "When Joseph woke from his sleep, he did as the Lord commanded him and took Mary as his wife," which sounds simple and clear, except we have to remember that Matthew was writing about all this eighty years after it happened. It was Matthew's story to write, but it wasn't Matthew's decision to make. What must it have been like for Joseph to settle on the reasonable plan of verse 19 only then to have the unreasonable dream of verse 20? If he follows his verse-19 plan, he takes control of his life. If he obeys his verse-20 dream, he loses control of his life. The plan he settled on in verse 19 makes good sense. *Well, I learned that Mary was expecting this baby, and I knew it wasn't mine. Yes, I know what the Bible says about punishing her, but I didn't want to hurt her. I heard she was going somewhere else, maybe over to Bethlehem, to have the baby. I don't know.* That's the verse-19 plan, and Joseph can explain it to anyone. Then there's the verse-20 dream, which Joseph can explain to no one. *Yes, I know that Mary is expecting. No, it's not my child. But you see, I had this dream, and in my dream I saw this angel, and the angel said Mary had conceived this child by an act of God. The Holy . . . no really, listen to me . . . the Holy Spirit came over her and . . . I don't know. All I know is that God told me to marry Mary and that the child will be special and that's what I'm doing.* Poor Joseph . . . he has already gone the second mile, constructing a plan that is kinder than what the Bible demands. Now he is being told to go further even than what common sense allows. And worse yet, it came to him in a dream. A dream, mind you. What he had in verse 19 was a careful, reasonable plan he could defend to anybody. What he gets in verse 20 is a thin, fleeting dream he can explain to nobody. Poor Joseph.

If I'm Joseph, I'm probably sticking with my verse-19 plan. This verse-20 dream makes no sense. If I've got to choose between basing my future on a reasonable plan I settled on while wide-awake or a risky dream I stumbled on while I was half-asleep, I'm probably not going with the dream. A dream is too fleeting, too uncertain, too thin, odd, and unsubstantial a thing upon which to base an entire future. You go around choosing dreams over plans, and the next thing you know you're hearing voices, feeling tugs, obeying nudges. You end up doing things no one understands, going to dangerous places, and embracing lost causes and questionable people. You could even end up bathing lepers like Mother Teresa, giving all your clothes to poor folks like Francis of Assisi did, or getting yourself shot to death like that young civil rights worker Jonathan Myrick Daniels over in Alabama thirty-something years ago.

If you think I'm exaggerating the danger of obeying a dream, just follow Joseph around some December. Joseph chose the dream he had in verse 20 over the plan he made in verse 19, and if you follow him around any December, what you'll discover is that, every Christmas, Joseph ends up in a cow barn/homeless shelter standing around with a bunch of poor folks tending to a baby that isn't even his.

Now what kind of place is that to spend Christmas? You can't have Christmas in a place like that, can you? We wouldn't want to end up like that, would we?

Amen.

CHAPTER 18

The Other Half

⁶⁰When many of his disciples heard it, they said, "This teaching is difficult; who can accept it?" ⁶¹But Jesus, being aware that his disciples were complaining about it, said to them, "Does this offend you? ⁶²Then what if you were to see the Son of Man ascending to where he was before? ⁶³It is the spirit that gives life; the flesh is useless. The words that I have spoken to you are spirit and life. ⁶⁴But among you there are some who do not believe." For Jesus knew from the first who were the ones that did not believe, and who was the one that would betray him. ⁶⁵And he said, "For this reason I have told you that no one can come to me unless it is granted by the Father." ⁶⁶Because of this many of his disciples turned back and no longer went about with him. ⁶⁷So Jesus asked the twelve, "Do you also wish to go away?" ⁶⁸Simon Peter answered him, "Lord, to whom can we go? You have the words of eternal life. ⁶⁹We have come to believe and know that you are the Holy One of God." (John 6:60-69)

By the time you get to the end of John 6, folks are slowly making their way toward the exits. Somewhere around verse 60 they start gathering up their things and heading for the parking lot. A few are staying, but most are leaving. The crowd is dwindling because they are so bothered by what Jesus is saying. John 6:60 sums up the problem this way:

"When many of Jesus' disciples heard his words, they said, 'This teaching is difficult; who can accept it?' And Jesus, being aware that his disciples were complaining about it, said to them, 'Does this offend you?'" All of which prepares us for the crowded exit we find in John 6:66: "Many of Jesus' disciples turned back and no longer went with him."

This was one of those times when Jesus lost more people than he kept. It often happened that way. As soon as one part of his message drew a crowd, another part of his message scattered them. With part of his life he healed the sick and fed the hungry and helped the hurting. That's the half of Jesus that drew a crowd. But with the other part of his life, Jesus called people to lay down their own self-interest, security, and protectionism in order to find the life God meant them to live. And that's the half of Jesus' message that kept his approval ratings barely in the double digits.

That fact has not been lost on the churches of the world. Those of us who are in the church know which parts of the gospel can gather a crowd, and we know which parts can lose a crowd. In fact, it's almost as though there are two gospels. There's a user-friendly, popular, North American gospel we offer to attract people on the principle that "We have to do whatever it takes to get people in the door so they can hear the gospel." But the problem, of course, is that if we use a diluted version of the gospel to "get people in," we cannot later unveil the real gospel and say, "Oh, by the way, this is really what we were asking you to sign up for. We attracted you to our church with a message that fit in just fine with the conventional wisdom of American culture. We appealed to your sense of comfort and ease and consumerism by pointing out all our church had to offer you in the way of programs and activities and such, but what we were actually inviting you to is a gospel that calls you to let go of your own self-interest and give yourself away as Jesus gave himself away. But we thought that might not get you in the door, so we saved that for now." A church can't do that. So what happens is that many churches, in a desire to get and keep a crowd, simply don't deal much in the hard sayings of Jesus that don't fit with the conventional wisdom on which we have built our lives.

Many churches have a Christianity that is more about Paul than it is about Jesus, because Paul's letters can be made to fit a little better with what we already think, while Jesus' words will utterly shatter the status quo. For example, there is Matthew 5:39-45, "Do not resist an evildoer. If anyone strikes you on the right cheek, turn the other also. If anyone wants to sue for your coat, give them your cloak also. Give to everyone who begs from you, and do not refuse anyone who wants to borrow from you. Love your enemies and pray for those who hurt you." Or Luke 6:22, "Blessed are you when people hate you and revile you on my account, but woe to you when everyone speaks well of you." Or Luke 14:33, "None of you can become my disciple if you do not give up all your possessions." You put all that together, and you know what kind of Lord we have . . . a Lord who does not fit with the conventional wisdom and prevailing assumptions that guide and govern our lives. That's the hard half of Jesus, the half that fills the exits early.

The British poet Algernon Swinburne, upon returning from church one Sunday, was asked how the preacher did, to which Swinburne offered the severe assessment, "For tender minds he served up half a Christ."[1] It is the church's job to serve up the whole Jesus, not just the half with which we feel most at home. After all, there aren't two gospels. There is only one. There is one gospel, and it is composed of all that Jesus said and did. Half of it comforts us. Half of it troubles us. This is the nature of the gospel. The gospel gives to us all that we need, and it demands from us all that we are.[2] It fills us with peace and it disrupts our lives. This is all reminiscent of a story in Barbara Brown Taylor's book, *Home by Another Way*, in which she writes,

> Several years ago I attended a weekend retreat where the opening exercise was to tell a story about someone who had been Christ for us in our lives. One after the other, there were stories of comfort, compassion, and rescue. The conference room turned into a church, where we settled into the warmth of each other's company. Jesus our friend was there with us and all was right with the world, until this one woman stood up and said, "Well, the first thing I thought about when I tried to think who had been Christ

to me was, 'Who in my life has told me the truth so clearly that I wanted to kill him for it?'" She burst our bubble, but she was onto something vitally important that most of us would be glad to forget: namely, that the Christ is not only the one who comforts and rescues us. The Christ is also the one who challenges and upsets us.[2]

It's the truth, isn't it? The same Lord who comforts our most troubling fears also troubles our most comfortable ideas. Oh, to be sure, we can fix that. People do it all the time. We can smooth all this out and make Jesus manageable. The problem is that if we do smooth the gospel out and make it fit with the way we already think, then we'll be left with only about half a gospel . . . and half a Christ.
Amen.

NOTES

[1] I heard this phrase attributed to Algernon Swinburne by the late John W. Carlton.

[2] This sentence is not original with me. I have heard it several times in various versions.

[3] Barbara Brown Taylor, *Home by Another Way* (Boston: Cowley Publications, 1999), 42-43.

CHAPTER 19

Still Surprising

"When the Son of Man comes in his glory, and all the angels with him, then he will sit on the throne of his glory. ³²All the nations will be gathered before him, and he will separate people one from another as a shepherd separates the sheep from the goats, ³³and he will put the sheep at his right hand and the goats at the left. ³⁴Then the king will say to those at his right hand, 'Come, you that are blessed by my Father, inherit the kingdom prepared for you from the foundation of the world; ³⁵for I was hungry and you gave me food, I was thirsty and you gave me something to drink, I was a stranger and you welcomed me, ³⁶I was naked and you gave me clothing, I was sick and you took care of me, I was in prison and you visited me.' ³⁷Then the righteous will answer him, 'Lord, when was it that we saw you hungry and gave you food, or thirsty and gave you something to drink? ³⁸And when was it that we saw you a stranger and welcomed you, or naked and gave you clothing? ³⁹And when was it that we saw you sick or in prison and visited you?' ⁴⁰And the king will answer them, 'Truly I tell you, just as you did it to one of the least of these who are members of my family, you did it to me.' ⁴¹Then he will say to those at his left hand, 'You that are accursed, depart from me into the eternal fire prepared for the devil and his angels; ⁴²for I was hungry and you gave me no food, I was thirsty and you gave me nothing to drink, ⁴³I was a stranger and you did not welcome me, naked and you did not give me clothing, sick and in prison and you did not visit me.'

44 Then they also will answer, 'Lord, when was it that we saw you hungry or thirsty or a stranger or naked or sick or in prison, and did not take care of you?' 45 Then he will answer them, 'Truly I tell you, just as you did not do it to one of the least of these, you did not do it to me.' 46 And these will go away into eternal punishment, but the righteous into eternal life." (Matthew 25:31-46)

Everyone in the room was surprised. When the king said to the ones on the right, "When you did it to one of the least of these, you did it to me," they were astonished. And when the king said to the ones on the left, "When you did not do it to one of the least of these, you did not do it to me," they were stunned. By the end of the story, everyone in the room was surprised. Those who fed the hungry, visited the prisoners, and comforted the sick entered into eternal life shaking their heads in amazement: "I had no idea. I never saw Christ in the soup line." The others, who did not feed the hungry, visit the prisoners, or comfort the sick went away to eternal punishment shaking their heads in amazement also: "How was I to know that it was Christ who needed a place to live? If I'd known it was Jesus, I would've helped. Who knew?"

Everyone in the room was surprised. But what's really surprising is that after all these years, this old, old story is still surprising. We've been hearing this story for as long as we can remember. Yet, the way it describes Judgment Day still leaves us surprised. After all, the popular Christianity that dominates the landscape of the religious world in which many of us live reduces judgment and eternity down to a single question: "Did you ask Jesus into your heart?" If the answer is yes, you go to eternal life. If the answer is no, you go to eternal punishment. You either accepted Jesus or you didn't, and you're in or you're out based on that and that alone. That is the only perspective on salvation many of us have ever heard. And there is plenty of Scripture to support that view. There is a verse in John 3: "Those who believe in Christ are not condemned, but those who do not believe are condemned already, because they have not believed in the only son of God." And another in Romans 10: "One believes with the heart and is justified, and one confesses with the mouth and is saved." And another in Ephesians 2: "By grace you have been saved through faith, and this is not your own doing; it is the gift of God, not the result of works." All of those verses, and others like them, are in the Bible. But Matthew 25 is also in the Bible, and in Matthew 25 the great issue on Judgment Day is an entirely different set of questions; questions that ask not what we have believed or decided about Jesus, but how we have responded to the most vulnerable of God's children. And those questions, much to our surprise, are not some sort of "star in your crown," extra credit, bonus questions. Rather, they are presented as the basis upon which our eternal destiny will be determined. According to Matthew 25:31-46, how we responded to God's most vulnerable children will be central, not peripheral; primary, not secondary; essential, not extra. According to Matthew 25:31-46, the big question we will face on Judgment Day will be this: How did we respond to God's most vulnerable, needy, lonely, poor, helpless, hurting children?

That is what the passage says. About that there is no question. The question, of course, is "What does it mean?" It's a parable, so like all parables it is filled with rich, poetic, storytelling images, all to be taken seriously but not literally. After all, if we were to take this parable literally, it would mean we are saved by works, not by grace. If we take this parable from Matthew 25 literally, everyone who fails to help the hungry and homeless is going to hell. But that doesn't ring true to the ways of God. So we don't take this story literally. It's a parable, of course, so we mustn't take it literally. But it is a parable of Jesus, so, of course, we must take it seriously. That alone would be enough to transform our thinking and revolutionize our lives. Try taking this seriously: How we respond to the most vulnerable, helpless, poor, sick, marginalized, lonely people in our city and our world is not a little bonus question buried in the footnotes. Rather, it is an enormous, fundamental, basic issue at the center of our relationship to God.

Taking Matthew 25 seriously is enough to make us look more closely, care more deeply, give more freely, and live more lovingly toward whomever is most in need. And that alone would be enough to transform our lives in ways that might leave everyone who knows us . . . surprised.

Amen.

CHAPTER 20

The Biggest Verse of All

³⁴When the Pharisees heard that he had silenced the Sadducees, they gathered together, ³⁵and one of them, a lawyer, asked him a question to test him. ³⁶"Teacher, which commandment in the law is the greatest?" ³⁷He said to him, "'You shall love the Lord your God with all your heart, and with all your soul, and with all your mind.' ³⁸This is the greatest and first commandment. ³⁹And a second is like it: 'You shall love your neighbor as yourself.' ⁴⁰On these two commandments hang all the law and the prophets." (Matthew 22:34-40)

The more I read the Bible, the more I understand what Sister Husband was talking about. Sister Husband is a character in a novel called *Where the Heart Is.* Sister Husband's calling in life is to give away Bibles. It's a noble pursuit, but she goes about it in a rather odd way. She never gives anybody a whole Bible or even a pocket New Testament. Sister Husband only gives people a single book of the Bible at most, usually just a chapter. Her rationale for that piecemeal distribution of Scripture goes like this: "Folks read too much of the Bible, they get confused. Read a little of the Bible and you're just a little confused. Read a lot and you're a lot confused. That's why I just give out a chapter at a time."[1]

Sister Husband has a point. It does get confusing sometimes, reading the Bible. The reason for the confusion is that the Bible sometimes speaks with more than one voice. If you have read much of the Bible, you have discovered the Bible's varied voices. It is those varied biblical voices that keep getting us caught in *wellyeahbut* conversations. You are, perhaps, familiar with the *wellyeahbut* category of biblical interpretation. It usually goes something like this: One person says the Bible supports capital punishment because Deuteronomy 19:21 says, "Life for life, eye for eye, tooth for tooth," but another person says, "Well, yeah, but what about Romans 12:17, which says 'Do not repay anyone evil for evil'?" One person says Christianity has replaced Judaism because Ephesians 2:15 says, "Christ has abolished the law," but another person says, "Well, yeah, but what about Matthew 5:17, where Jesus says, 'Do not think that I have come to abolish the law'?" One person will say women cannot be pastors because 1 Corinthians 14:34 says for women to be silent in the church, but another person says "Well, yeah, but what about Acts 2:17-18, which says God is pouring out God's spirit on God's sons and God's daughters so that both the sons and the daughters can proclaim God's word?" One person will say the church can support war because Romans 13:4 says the government wields the sword for God, but another person will say, "Well, yeah, but what about Matthew 5:39 and 44, where Jesus says, 'Resist not an evildoer. If anyone strikes you on the right cheek turn the other also . . . love your enemies'?" One person will say the only issue that will matter on Judgment Day is how we responded to Jesus, because John 3:17 says those who do not believe in the name of the only Son of God are condemned, but another person will say, "Well, yeah, but in Matthew 25:31-46, the Bible says what happens to us on Judgment Day will depend entirely upon how we responded to the hungry, the thirsty, the stranger, the patient, and the prisoner." One person will say we should only give aid to the working poor because 2 Thessalonians 3:10 says, "Anyone unwilling to work should not eat," but another person will say, "Well, yeah, but that doesn't match up with Matthew 5:42 where Jesus says, 'Give to everyone who begs from you, and do not refuse anyone who wants to borrow from you.'"

It's a fact, and there's no denying it. The Bible sometimes speaks with more than one voice on the same subject. We simply cannot read the whole Bible and miss that fact. So what does it mean for those of us who love the Bible and long to interpret it truthfully and live by it carefully? Well, for starters it means no single verse of Scripture should ever be interpreted in isolation from the rest of the Bible. Rather, any single verse of Scripture should be interpreted in conversation with the rest of the Bible. Of course, we don't always interpret Scripture, nor should we. Sometimes we simply read the Bible for comfort or guidance or strength. But sometimes we do interpret Scripture, and when we do, we must interpret any single passage of Scripture not in isolation from, but in conversation with, the rest of the Bible.

The problem is, once we do that—once we do the hard work of careful biblical interpretation where every passage is interpreted in conversation with, not in isolation from, the rest of the Bible—we then must decide which Bible verse will carry the day, which word of Scripture will have more authority over our lives and which will have less. *But aren't all the words of Scripture supposed to have equal authority?* Well, that's what some say, and it is certainly a nice-sounding theory, but careful speech requires us to confess that every word of Scripture does not have equal authority. The next time someone tells you they believe that every word of Scripture is of equal authority, ask them to show you their closet. It should be rather small and nearly empty, of course, because Luke 3:11 says that whoever has two coats must give one to someone who has none, not to mention Luke 14:33, "None of you can become my disciples if you do not give up all your possessions." Or ask them if they are absolute pacifists (Matthew 5:39, "Do not resist an evildoer.") Or ask them if they steer clear of beauty parlors and jewelry stores (1 Timothy 2:9, "Women should dress themselves modestly . . . not with their hair braided, or with gold, pearls or expensive clothes.") It's a fact, and people need to face it. Even those of us who would like to embrace, as a religious conviction, the idea that every word of scripture weighs the same work our way through the Bible embracing the verses that support our politics and our economics and dismissing the verses that don't fit with the way our life works. It's a fact, and careful speech requires us to say it.

Why not simply speak the truth? The truth is the Bible holds the most comforting, challenging, life-changing words in all the world, but the Bible's words do not all weigh the same. It isn't just that they don't. The truth is, they can't. You can go with "An eye for an eye, and a tooth for a tooth" or you can go with "Do not repay evil for evil," but you can't do both. You can go with "Let women be silent in the church" or you can go with "In Christ there is neither male or female," but you can't do both. You can go with Numbers 31, which justifies violence against enemies, or you can go with Matthew 5, which calls for love toward enemies, but you can't do both. So, yes, it is true; we do finally have to choose which verses of Scripture will have authority over our lives. Every word in the Bible does not weigh the same.

Which brings us to Matthew 22:34-40. When the inquirer approached Jesus and asked, "Which commandment is the most important one of all?" Jesus had his chance to say, "They are all equally important, because they are all Scripture, and every word of Scripture is of equal importance." Instead, Jesus said some words of Scripture really are more important than others: "'You shall love the Lord your God with all your heart, and with all your soul and with all your mind.' This is the greatest commandment," said Jesus. "And the second most important commandment is 'You shall love your neighbor as yourself.'" And then Jesus said, "On these two commandments hang all the law and the prophets." And with that, Jesus gave his hearers a standard by which to interpret everything else in the Bible. The standard of biblical interpretation was, according to Jesus, love for God and love for others. "Everything else hangs on that," said Jesus, passing on the chance to say that all Scripture is equally important and choosing instead to acknowledge that some words of Scripture weigh more than others, and declaring love for God and love for others as the weightiest words of all.

So that's it. That's the big one, the biggest Bible verse of them all. Among the Bible's many voices, that is the voice that gets to have the final say. It doesn't settle all the *wellyeahbuts* or give us an easy formula for declaring "the biblical position" on every issue of the day, but it does give us a place to begin in our efforts to interpret the Bible's varied voices. "Love God with all that is in you and love others as yourself" is the first word, according to Jesus, and the last. This is where we begin, and this is where we end, with the Bible's biggest verse and weightiest word: Love God with all that is in you, and love others as you love yourself. Every other word of Scripture will have to be measured by that standard. Or, as Jesus said, "Everything else hangs on this."

Somewhere in the distance is the soft echo of T. S. Eliot's verse,

We shall not cease from exploration
And the end of all our exploring
Will be to arrive where we started
And to know the place for the first time.[2]

To speak truthfully about the Bible and live carefully by the Bible is never to cease listening, learning, repenting, growing, changing, and exploring. But at the end of it all, at the end of all our exploring, we finally arrive where we started. We finally come back to this: "Love God with all that is in you, and love others as you love yourself." Everything finally comes back to this.

Amen.

NOTES

[1] Billie Letts, *Where the Heart Is* (New York: Warner Books, 1995), 18.

[2] *T. S. Eliot, The Complete Poems and Plays* (New York: Harcourt, Bruce, and Company, 1950), 145.

CHAPTER 21

We Ordain Women Because We Baptize Girls

27 As many of you as were baptized into Christ have clothed yourselves with Christ. 28 There is no longer Jew or Greek, there is no longer slave or free, there is no longer male and female; for all of you are one in Christ Jesus. 29 And if you belong to Christ, then you are Abraham's offspring, heirs according to the promise. (Galatians 3:27-29)

Rarely has anyone thrown such cold water on such a tall wall as did Paul when he wrote, "As many of you as were baptized into Christ have clothed yourselves with Christ. There is no longer Jew or Greek, there is no longer slave or free, there is no longer male and female, for all of you are one in Christ Jesus." One imagines that Paul's words about baptism made quite a splash in Galatia. The idea that the walls of race, class, and gender are washed away in the water of baptism ran counter to the conventional wisdom of Paul's world, conventional wisdom that was captured in a popular "men-only" prayer that went like this: "Blessed art thou, O Lord our God, who hast not made me a Gentile. Blessed art thou, O Lord our God, who hast not made me a slave. Blessed art thou, O Lord our God, who hast not made me a woman." What Paul told the Galatians was that, in the water of baptism, those divisions are swept away. "As many of you as were baptized into Christ have clothed yourselves with Christ. There is no longer Jew or Greek, there is no longer slave or free, there is no longer male or female, for all of you are one in Christ Jesus." Paul told the church at Galatia that they could not embrace the water of baptism while also holding on to the walls of division. Their neat, settled, familiar categories of race, class, and gender had been washed away in the water of baptism.[1]

If that's what Galatians 3:27-29 meant for them then, what does it mean for us now? I believe it means now what it meant then, which is that, in the water of baptism, our culture's walls of division are washed away. Race, class, and gender remain as human realities, but for those who have been baptized, they can no longer be relevant to who's in or who's out, who leads by serving or who serves by leading. Men are still male and women are still female, but in the baptized family of faith, in the church of Jesus Christ, it just doesn't matter. That's what Galatians 3:27-29 means.

So why have some baptized Christians so steadfastly maintained their denial of certain roles in the church to people based on nothing more than the fact they happen to have been born female? I think they would say, "Because of what the Bible says." After all, in 1 Corinthians 14:34-35, the Bible says, "Women should keep silent in the church. They are not permitted to speak, but should be subordinate. If there is anything they want to know they should ask their husbands at home. It is shameful for a woman to speak in church." And then there is 1 Timothy 2:11-12, which says, "Let a woman learn in silence, in full submission. I permit no woman to teach a man." So there you go. That's what the Bible says. End of story. Right? Well, not exactly. The same Bible that gives us 1 Corinthians 14:34-35 and 1 Timothy 2:11-12 also gives us Acts 2:17-18, which says, "Thus says the Lord, I will pour out my spirit upon all flesh, and your sons and your daughters shall prophesy." Here, God specifically includes daughters and sisters as preachers and proclaimers. Then, of course, there is 1 Corinthians 11:5, "Any woman who prays or prophesies with her head unveiled disgraces her head." Obviously, Paul is expecting women to lead worship, otherwise why would he establish a dress code for women worship leaders?

Here, as in other cases, the Bible speaks with more than one voice. That's why we must always interpret any single passage of Scripture in conversation with, not in isolation from, the rest of the Bible. When it comes to the roles of women in the church, the Bible does not speak with one seamless, homogenized, unanimous voice. If all we have to go on are the words on the page, then the Bible is pretty much in a tie. (With itself!)

So what breaks the tie? For me, the tie was broken many years ago by the boundary-shattering, wall-removing, all-including Spirit of Christ. But if the Spirit of Jesus is too subjective, if we must limit ourselves to that which is written in black and white on the pages of Scripture, I would say that the tiebreaker is Galatians 3:27-29, which tells us that in the church, the world's distinctions of race, class, and gender have been washed away in the water of baptism.

Based on all of that, I offer this modest proposal: If anyone should ever ask why your church ordains women, just tell them that, based on a careful reading of the Bible, your church discovered that if you were going to refuse ordination to women, you'd first have to refuse baptism to girls because Galatians 3 says that once a person has been baptized, their gender is no more an issue in the church than the color of their eyes or their hair or their skin. Tell them that based on a careful reading of Galatians 3:27-29, your church ordains men *and* women because your church baptizes boys *and* girls.

Amen.

NOTE

[1] See John Timmer's sermon "Owning Up to Baptism," in *A Chorus of Witnesses*, ed. Thomas E. Long and Cornelius Platinga Jr. (GrandRapids: Eerdmons Publishing Company, 1994), 279-85.

CHAPTER 22

No Full End

*¹⁸"Your ways and your doings have brought this upon you. This is your doom;
how bitter it is! It has reached your very heart." ¹⁹My anguish, my anguish! I
writhe in pain! Oh, the walls of my heart! My heart is beating wildly; I cannot
keep silent; for I hear the sound of the trumpet, the alarm of war. ²⁰Disaster
overtakes disaster, the whole land is laid waste. Suddenly my tents are destroyed,
my curtains in a moment. ²¹How long must I see the standard, and hear the
sound of the trumpet? ²²"For my people are foolish, they do not know me; they
are stupid children, they have no understanding. They are skilled in doing evil,
but do not know how to do good." ²³I looked on the earth, and lo, it was waste
and void; and to the heavens, and they had no light. ²⁴I looked on the mountains, and lo, they were quaking, and all the hills moved to and fro. ²⁵I looked,
and lo, there was no one at all, and all the birds of the air had fled. ²⁶I looked,
and lo, the fruitful land was a desert, and all its cities were laid in ruins before
the LORD, before his fierce anger. ²⁷For thus says the LORD: The whole land
shall be a desolation; yet I will not make a full end. (Jeremiah 4:18-27)*

As you may have noticed, there appears to be a pattern in the Bible. It
begins at the beginning, in Genesis. And it ends at the end, in the
Revelation. The pattern first emerges in the garden of Eden, where
God warns Adam and Eve to steer clear of the off-limits tree, saying

that in the day they eat from that tree they will die. Dire predictions notwithstanding, they proceed to eat from the off-limits tree, so we expect them to die that day. But God doesn't kill them. Instead, God evicts them. But before God sends them away, God gives them a sign of grace: sturdier clothes to help them survive in the hard world that waits east of Eden.

Soon, Adam and Eve's sons are embroiled in a conflict that leads to Cain's murder of Abel. As punishment, Cain is consigned to wander as a homeless man in the unknown land of Nod. But even as God is sending Cain away, God gives him a sign of grace: the gift of a protective mark to help him make it in the land of Nod.

Then comes the flood, which destroys everything and everyone, except Noah's family and their floating zoo. As soon as the boat lands, God says, "I'm never going to do anything like that again. No matter how bad people get, I'll never again destroy everything and everybody." And as a reminder, God hangs out a rainbow, a sign of grace like Adam's clothes and Cain's mark.

And then, of course, there is Jonah, who refuses God's call, runs from God's tug, and gets in over his head. But God sends the huge fish so that Jonah can have a new day and another chance.

There seems to be a pattern here: a pattern of new days and new chances. The pattern marches on: In the book of Isaiah, God indicts God's people for their sinful ways but then says, "Do not be afraid; I will blot out your transgressions; I will not remember your sins." In the book of Zephaniah, God is so angry with God's people that God says, "I am going to sweep away all humanity from the face of the earth." But by the end of the book, God says, "Do not be afraid. I will renew you with my love." In the book of Hosea, God says, "The more I call to my people, the further they go from me." Their refusal of God causes God to consider rejecting them, but then God says, "How can I give them up? I will heal their disloyalty and love them freely."

There seems to be a pattern here, a pattern of new days and new chances. Based on that pattern, it appears that God is never through, finished, or done with anyone.

Cross over into the New Testament, and the pattern continues: The woman caught in adultery is told to sin no more and sent away to live in the light of forgiveness and grace. Peter fails miserably on the night of Jesus' trial but is given a new beginning at the after-Easter breakfast. Jesus tells the parables in Luke 15 to show that God will not rest until every lost sinner is found and welcomed and rejoiced over. Paul writes to the Romans that nothing in the whole wide world will ever be able to separate us from the love of God. And then, on the last page of the last book of the Bible, in Revelation 21:25, the Bible says the gates of pearl are all open all the time. God's got gates, and they're all wide open forever. That, of course, fits the pattern; the pattern of God; the Bible-long pattern of unending love and unfailing grace that winds its way from Genesis to Revelation.

That pattern is captured in a tiny phrase from the book of Jeremiah. It is a phrase so small that it's easy to miss, but it holds a truth so big that you can fit the whole pattern of God inside its three simple syllables. I'm talking about that odd little phrase in Jeremiah 4:27, "no full end." God has been lamenting, through the prophet Jeremiah, about how sinful God's people have become and about how severe the consequences will be for their rebellion, and then, in the midst of those fierce indictments, God says, "But I will make no full end." In the midst of that long recital of darkness and doom, there is this little sign of grace; like the clothes for Adam and the mark for Cain and the rainbow for Noah and the fish for Jonah and the party for the prodigal and the gates stuck open forever; like all those hints, signs, and clues of grace and forgiveness, there is this little phrase in Jeremiah 4:27: "no full end." This God will not make a full, complete, absolute end of these people, because this is the God of new days, new chances, endless love, and undaunted grace, the God of "no full ends."

Kirby Godsey captured it best when he said, "God will always let us leave, but God will never let us go."[1] It's true. Because we are free to make even the most terrible choices, God will always let us turn away and walk away and destroy our lives and the lives of those we love. In other words, God will always let us leave. But the rest of the truth is that God will never let us go, because God is free also: free to be as loving and forgiving and full of grace as God wants to be. God is as free to forgive as we are to sin. God is not bound to love and forgive only up to the limits we have set for God with our doctrines and beliefs. And, based on that Bible-wide, cover-to-cover, front-to-back, Genesis-to-Revelation pattern that keeps reemerging in Scripture, it would appear that when it comes to giving grace, God has chosen to be something more than our doctrines have instructed God to be. It would appear that God may have chosen, even without our permission, to be the God of no full end.

I don't know if that is so, but if that should turn out to be the case, it would certainly fit the pattern.

Amen.

NOTE

[1] I once heard Dr. Godsey say that sentence in a sermon.

CHAPTER 23

. . . *And The Gates Never Close*

²²I saw no temple in the city, for its temple is the Lord God the Almighty and the Lamb. ²³And the city has no need of sun or moon to shine on it, for the glory of God is its light, and its lamp is the Lamb. ²⁴The nations will walk by its light, and the kings of the earth will bring their glory into it. ²⁵Its gates will never be shut by day—and there will be no night there. ²⁶People will bring into it the glory and the honor of the nations. ²⁷But nothing unclean will enter it, nor anyone who practices abomination or falsehood, but only those who are written in the Lamb's book of life.

¹Then the angel showed me the river of the water of life, bright as crystal, flowing from the throne of God and of the Lamb ²through the middle of the street of the city. On either side of the river is the tree of life with its twelve kinds of fruit, producing its fruit each month; and the leaves of the tree are for the healing of the nations. ³Nothing accursed will be found there any more. But the throne of God and of the Lamb will be in it, and his servants will worship him; ⁴they will see his face, and his name will be on their foreheads. ⁵And there will be no more night; they need no light of lamp or sun, for the Lord God will be their light, and they will reign forever and ever. (Revelation 21:22–22:5)

Several years ago I was standing in a grocery store checkout line when I became intrigued by a headline in the *Weekly World News*. The headline proclaimed, "Bible's Greatest Mysteries Solved." What with me being a preacher and all, I was especially eager to see what light the *Weekly World News* might cast on the many mysteries in the book of the Revelation. But, alas, while I did learn that a UFO was involved in the parting of the Red Sea (a fact that had somehow previously escaped my attention), I found no mention of the last book of the Bible. Apparently, even the *Weekly World News* theology department found the Revelation's many mysteries a bit too daunting to tackle. And who can blame them? After all, just think what you encounter when you wander around in the Revelation. In chapter 4, we meet creatures who have eyes in the backs of their heads. In chapter 6, the sun turns black, the moon turns red, and the stars turn loose. In chapter 13 there is a beast with a leopard's body, a bear's feet, and a lion's mouth. In chapter 19 there is a lake burning with fire, and in chapter 21 there is a city shining with gold. Those are just a few of the strange sights that mystify those who read the Revelation.

Needless to say, such mysterious images have prompted a wide array of interpretations, the most popular of which treats the Revelation as a series of predictions for the future, predictions that can be charted and calendared in a definite chronological sequence. This interpretation of the Revelation has given rise to an entire industry of books and movies about the end of time. It is assumed by millions to be the only way to interpret the Revelation. But, despite its huge popularity, we have to be careful with that view of the Revelation, because it tends to assign literal meaning to images that the author, John, offered as metaphors and pictures, not facts and figures. It is not safe to interpret John's revelation literally because John wasn't writing literally. John was writing in a style called "apocalyptic," which employs all sorts of colors and numbers and animals and images in poetic, lyrical, symbolic ways to communicate a central and significant message.

And what is the message John sought to tell? What is the meaning at the heart of the last book of the Bible? Our best hope to discover the answer to those questions is to begin by looking at the Revelation not as an intriguing puzzle written to be solved by twenty-first-century readers but as a pastoral letter written to be heard by first-century believers.[1] To read the Revelation is to read someone else's mail, in the same sense that we are reading someone else's mail when we read Paul's epistles.[2] Take, for example, Philippians and Galatians. Those letters have powerful messages for us, but they were not written to us or about us. Originally they were written to the Philippians and about the Galatians. The same principle holds when we read the Revelation. It has an enormous message for us, but it was not written to us or about us. It was written to a group of late first-century churches who were enduring a difficult time under a Roman emperor named Domitian. Domitian, who was emperor from AD 81 to 96, took the idea of "emperor worship" to new heights.[3] While he did not control who or what his subjects worshiped in private, he required that they bow to him as Lord in public. This, of course, presented a problem for serious followers of Jesus. Their one and only Lord was Christ. Thus, they could not, in good conscience, worship as Lord a government official. For their refusal to worship the emperor, they paid the price of persecution. That was the situation in the mid-nineties, when it appears that the Revelation was written. From his place of exile where he was sent for his own commitment to Christ as Lord, John wrote a letter to be read in the churches where believers were suffering for the faith under Domitian. That letter is the Revelation. In it John described, in lyrical, symbolic, picture-book language, a vision in which the church's suffering and struggle will ultimately be turned to triumph and joy by the power and goodness of God. In fact, if you want to see what the main message of the Revelation is, turn to Revelation 11:15, "The kingdoms of this world have become the kingdoms of our God and of his Christ, and he shall reign forever and ever." That is the message of the Revelation, compressed to a single sentence. All the hurtful, harmful, evil powers of this world will some-day be swallowed up into the kingdom of God, and God's goodness and grace will rule and reign forever. Or turn to Revelation 14:12-13: "Here is a call for the endurance of the saints. Keep the command-ments of God and hold fast to the faith of Jesus. Blessed are the dead who die from now on in the Lord. They will rest from their labors, and their works will follow them."

That was John's main message to his church, and it is his great lesson for us: "Hold on. Don't give up or give in. Remember whose you are and who you are. Practice your faith, no matter what, even if it gets you killed, because ultimately your future is in God's hands and your labor will not be lost, futile, or in vain." That is the message of the Revelation. It is a word of hope for those who struggle and stumble and stagger through trials and troubles and temptations. John has seen a vision of ultimate triumph and joy. He has had a glimpse of what awaits us beyond the struggles of life, when we will finally be welcomed into God's unhindered presence, where there will be no more sorrow or crying or pain, no more anything to fear or dread.

On the final pages of the Revelation, John describes that wonderful home for which we are headed as being like a city coming down out of heaven. In John's vision, it is a beautiful city, shiny as gold. Among its many remarkable features are its gates. There is a wall that surrounds the city, and it has twelve gates; three on the east, three on the north, three on the west, and three on the south. They are made of pearl, so they must be nice. But listen to this: "The city has a great high wall with twelve gates . . . . Each of the gates is a single pearl . . . . The gates will never be shut by day—and there will be no night there" (Revelation 21:12, 21, 25). A dozen gates made of pearl, but not a one of them works! They won't close. Twelve gates, and they're all open in all directions all the time. Wide open. Always. Forever.

What might that mean? Among the Revelation's many images and pictures, what might the image of a dozen gates wide open in all directions mean? I'm not sure. To say with certainty what the open gates mean would be to violate Romans 12:16 ("Do not claim to be wiser than you are"). I can't say for sure. I would like to believe that a dozen gates open forever in all directions are a sign that God's grace will not give up until all have come in and come home, but then there are all those other verses in the Bible that point to the final separation of some from the kingdom of God, verses such as Revelation 21:27, " . . . Nothing unclean will enter [the city of God], nor anyone who practices abomination or falsehood, but only those who are written in the Lamb's book of life."

So what can we say with certainty about all those gates open forever in all directions? Perhaps only that they fill us with hope; the hope that ultimately, finally, God's goodness and grace will not be defeated, but that ultimately, finally, the will of God will be done. "For it is not the will of the Father that any should perish, but that all should come to repentance" (2 Peter 3:9).

Wouldn't that be something? Wouldn't it be wonderful if God's ultimate will were ultimately accomplished? Dare we hope such a hope? There are arguments against such a hope, among them Christian traditions and a large lake of fire in the same Revelation that gives us those wide-open gates. But, on the other hand, God has a long history of going beyond what anyone dreamed or imagined God would do. So who's to say what God might yet do?

Amen.

NOTES

[1] For this way of thinking about the Revelation, see M. Eugene Boring, *Revelation* (Louisville, John Knox, 1989), 1-62.

[2] For the phrase "reading someone else's mail" as a way of thinking about biblical letters, I am indebted to Fred Craddock.

[3] Boring, *Revelation*, 21.

CHAPTER 24

Glad to Be Wrong

¹ *"For the kingdom of heaven is like a landowner who went out early in the morning to hire laborers for his vineyard.* ² *After agreeing with the laborers for the usual daily wage, he sent them into his vineyard.* ³ *When he went out about nine o'clock, he saw others standing idle in the marketplace;* ⁴ *and he said to them, 'You also go into the vineyard, and I will pay you whatever is right.' So they went.* ⁵ *When he went out again about noon and about three o'clock, he did the same.* ⁶ *And about five o'clock he went out and found others standing around; and he said to them, 'Why are you standing here idle all day?'* ⁷ *They said to him, 'Because no one has hired us.' He said to them, 'You also go into the vineyard.'* ⁸ *When evening came, the owner of the vineyard said to his manager, 'Call the laborers and give them their pay, beginning with the last and then going to the first.'* ⁹ *When those hired about five o'clock came, each of them received the usual daily wage.* ¹⁰ *Now when the first came, they thought they would receive more; but each of them also received the usual daily wage.* ¹¹ *And when they received it, they grumbled against the landowner,* ¹² *saying, 'These last worked only one hour, and you have made them equal to us who have borne the burden of the day and the scorching heat.'* ¹³ *But he replied to one of them, 'Friend, I am doing you no wrong; did you not agree with me for the usual daily wage?* ¹⁴ *Take what belongs to you and go; I choose to give to this last the same as I give to you.* ¹⁵ *Am I not allowed to do what I choose with*

what belongs to me? Or are you envious because I am generous?' [16] *So the last will be first, and the first will be last." (Matthew 20:1-16)*

There's not much middle ground in Matthew 20:1-16. By the end of the parable, everybody on the page is either very glad or very mad. No wonder. After all, some worked overtime and others worked part-time, but everybody was paid the same. So the last-minute part-timers were mighty glad, but the all-day over-timers were pretty mad; mad enough that they descended on the landowner to cry "Unfair!" and plead their case. And that, of course, sets up the moment when the parable produces its punch line, which is traveling in the landowner's response to the angry all-day workers: "I am doing you no wrong. Did you not agree with me for the usual daily wage? Take what belongs to you and go. I choose to give to these last workers the same as I give to you. Am I not allowed to do what I choose with what belongs to me? Or are you envious because I am generous?"

And with that the story ends. Some are glad, some are mad, and we are left, once again, to respond to this odd parable that always leaves us a little off- balance. Even though we know that the story is not really about pay scales and labor relations, we still want to find those all-day workers and slip them a twenty because, deep down inside, we're on their side. But of course, the workers' plight is only there to draw us into the story, and the story is only there to draw us into the truth, the truth about the kingdom of heaven. The parable tells us what it is really about in the very first line: "The kingdom of heaven is like a landowner who went out early in the morning to hire laborers for his vineyards." That's what the strange little story is really about, according to the one who told it. And if this story is really about what the kingdom of heaven is like, then the point of the story is actually pretty clear. The point of the story is that, in God's kingdom, God can give God's grace to anyone God chooses, with or without our approval. The point of the story is that God will give us all the grace we ever dreamed of, and God will also give the same abundant grace to those we thought would not be as welcome as we in the kingdom of God.

That is the point of the story. The story warns us against becoming too certain that we know how God is going to relate to people who do differently than we. One of these days, we might get shocked. And, in the words of the parable, that will be the day when we might say, "But God, you can't make them equal to us. We worked and served and gave! We followed the right plan, but they didn't, so you can't let them in. You can't welcome them the way you welcome us." And in the words of the parable, God is going to say, "You've lived all your life with the understanding that you were mine and I was yours. And you know what? You were exactly right. So welcome home. The whole place is yours to enjoy. Now go enjoy it, while I also welcome in those whom you never expected to be the objects of my grace. What's that? Surely you are not angry because I am generous, are you?"

Well, actually, yes. Some of us who are in the church are a little angry at the thought of God being that good, that generous, that liberal, that free with grace and welcome and forgiveness, because, let's face it, those of us who are in the church are the all-day workers in the parable. We rise and shine and give and serve and believe and strive. God can't make those who didn't follow the plan equal to those of us who did. I mean, for one thing it isn't fair. And for another thing, we have doctrines to defend, and those doctrines say that those who followed the plan are in and those who didn't follow the plan are out and cannot be made equal to those who did follow the plan. That's what we've always been taught. That's what we've always believed. So yes, it does make us angry to think that God might be that generous, that liberal, that full of grace when judgment day comes, because the thought that God's welcome might turn out to be wider than we always assumed challenges things we've always believed about the way its going to be on judgment day. The thought that God's welcome might turn out to be wider than we always believed actually opens up the possibility that some of our long-settled assumptions might be wrong.

And that, of course, returns us to the point of the parable. The point of the parable is that the abundant generosity of God's grace is going to shock, surprise, and amaze everyone on judgment day. The parable suggests that, in the end, God will actually be free to do whatever God wants to do with God's grace, even if it means coloring outside the lines that we have drawn for God to follow. After all, God never has agreed to love and forgive and welcome people only up to the limits that popular Christian doctrine has set for God. We forget that God is nowhere on record as having agreed to be limited by what you and I have always believed. What if God has a different plan, a bigger idea than ours? According to the parable, God is going to give us all-day workers all the grace we've ever counted on, and God is also going to give the same welcome to folks we presently assume will not be equal to those of us who have followed the plan. According to the parable, the gates to the city of God might stand open wider and stay open longer than any of us would advise or approve or allow.

But that doesn't fit with the way we've always thought, so we don't like that. Exactly, which takes us back to the point of the parable. God is going to welcome people we would not have welcomed, and for that God does not need our permission or our approval. In the words of the parable, God can do whatever God chooses to do with that which belongs to God. And all the saving, forgiving, welcoming grace that ever was or ever will be always has and always will belong to God and God alone. If God turns out to be more generous with that grace than we had always assumed, we should just be glad we were wrong. We should be glad God didn't let what we had always believed keep God from being as good as God wanted to be. If it turns out that we've always been wrong about the limits we've set on God's saving grace, then that would be a case where being wrong should make us glad, not mad.

Or, in the words of the parable, surely we will not be angry because God is generous, will we? We won't be up there pushing on one of those big old gate-shaped pearls, trying to close a gate God left open too long, will we?

Amen.

There shall always be the Church and the World
And the heart of Man
Shivering and fluttering between them,
choosing and chosen.
Valiant, ignoble, dark and full of light
Swinging between Hell Gate and Heaven Gate
And the Gates of Hell shall not prevail.
Darkness now, then light.
—T. S. Eliot